Made | Simple™

Dinner

Publications International, Ltd.

Louis Weber, CEO
Publications International, Ltd.
8140 Lehigh Ave
Morton Grove, IL 60053

Pictured on the front cover: Chicken and Tomato Rotini *(page 30).*

Pictured on the back cover *(clockwise from top left):* Chicken and Sausage Jambalaya *(page 6),* Orecchiette with Sausage and Broccoli Rabe *(page 102)* and Chicken Adobo *(page 101).*

ISBN: 978-1-63938-999-5

Manufactured in China.

8 7 6 5 4 3 2 1

Microwave Cooking: Microwave ovens vary in wattage. Use the cooking times as guidelines and check for doneness before adding more time.

Let's get social!
@Publications_International
@PublicationsInternational
www.pilbooks.com

Contents

Skillet & One Pot Meals

Asian Chicken and Noodle Stir-Fry

MAKES 4 SERVINGS

- 8 ounces uncooked thin pad Thai rice noodles (⅛-inch wide)
- 1 tablespoon vegetable oil
- 1 pound boneless skinless chicken breasts, cut into 1×½-inch pieces
- 2 cloves garlic, minced
- 1 bottle (12 ounces) stir-fry sauce
- ¼ cup water
- 2 tablespoons packed brown sugar
- 1 package (16 ounces) frozen stir-fry vegetable blend (do not thaw)

1. Cook or soak noodles according to package directions until almost tender; drain.
2. Heat oil in wok or large skillet over high heat. Add chicken; cook and stir 4 minutes or until no longer pink. Add garlic; cook and stir 30 seconds. Remove chicken to plate.
3. Add stir-fry sauce, water and brown sugar to wok, stirring to scrape up browned bits. Stir in noodles, vegetables and chicken; cook until vegetables are tender and noodles are saucy.

Chicken and Sausage Jambalaya

MAKES 6 TO 8 SERVINGS

- 1½ tablespoons vegetable oil, divided
- 12 ounces boneless skinless chicken breast, cut into 1-inch pieces
- 12 to 14 ounces andouille sausage or other smoked sausage, cut into ¼-inch slices
- 1 onion, chopped
- ½ red bell pepper, chopped
- ½ green bell pepper, chopped
- 1½ tablespoons Cajun seasoning
- 3 cloves garlic, minced
- ¾ teaspoon dried thyme
- 1 can (about 14 ounces) diced tomatoes
- 2 bay leaves
- ½ teaspoon salt
- 2¾ cups chicken broth
- 1½ cups uncooked rice
- Sliced green onions or chopped fresh parsley (optional)

1. Heat 1 tablespoon oil in large saucepan or Dutch oven over medium-high heat. Add chicken; cook about 5 minutes or until browned, stirring occasionally. Remove to plate.
2. Add remaining ½ tablespoon oil and sausage to saucepan; cook 5 minutes or until browned, stirring occasionally. Remove to plate with chicken. Add onion and bell peppers to saucepan; cook 3 minutes or until vegetables are softened, scraping up browned bits from bottom of saucepan. Add Cajun seasoning, garlic and thyme; cook and stir 1 minute. Add tomatoes, bay leaves and salt; mix well. Stir in broth, rice, chicken and sausage; bring to a boil.
3. Reduce heat to low; cover and cook 30 minutes or until rice is tender and liquid is absorbed. Stir rice; remove and discard bay leaves. Top with green onions, if desired.

Mexican Cauliflower and Bean Skillet

MAKES 4 TO 6 SERVINGS

- 1 teaspoon olive oil
- 3 cups coarsely chopped cauliflower
- ¾ teaspoon salt
- ½ medium yellow onion, chopped
- 1 green bell pepper, chopped
- 1 clove garlic, minced
- 1 teaspoon chili powder
- ¾ teaspoon ground cumin
- Pinch ground red pepper
- 1 can (about 15 ounces) black beans, rinsed and drained
- 1 cup (4 ounces) shredded Cheddar-Jack cheese
- Salsa and sour cream

1 Heat oil in large nonstick skillet over medium-high heat. Add cauliflower and salt; cook and stir 5 minutes. Add onion, bell pepper, garlic, chili powder, cumin and red pepper; cook and stir 5 minutes or until cauliflower is tender. Stir in beans; cook until beans are heated through. Remove from heat.

2 Sprinkle with cheese; fold gently and let stand until melted. Serve with salsa and sour cream.

Serving Suggestion

Serve over brown rice or with warm corn tortillas.

One-Pot Pasta with Sausage

MAKES 6 SERVINGS

- 1 tablespoon olive oil
- 1 pound smoked sausage (about 4 links), cut into ¼-inch slices
- 1 onion, chopped
- 1 tablespoon tomato paste
- 2 cloves garlic, minced
- 1½ teaspoons dried oregano
- ¼ teaspoon red pepper flakes
- 1 can (28 ounces) whole tomatoes, undrained, crushed with hands or coarsely chopped
- 3 cups water
- 1½ teaspoons salt
- 1 package (16 ounces) uncooked cellentani pasta
- 1½ cups frozen peas
- ½ cup shredded Parmesan cheese
- ⅓ cup shredded fresh basil, plus additional for garnish

1. Heat oil in large saucepan over medium-high heat. Add sausage; cook about 7 minutes or until browned, stirring occasionally. Add onion; cook and stir 5 minutes or until softened. Add tomato paste, garlic, oregano and red pepper flakes; cook and stir 1 minute. Add tomatoes with juice, water and salt; cook 2 minutes, stirring to scrape up browned bits. Stir in pasta; mix well.

2. Bring to a boil. Reduce heat to medium-low; cover and simmer 10 minutes or until pasta is al dente, stirring occasionally and adding additional water if sauce is dry. Stir in peas; cook and stir 2 minutes. Stir in cheese and ⅓ cup basil. Cover and let stand 2 minutes. Garnish with additional basil.

Variation

You can substitute 1 pound uncooked Italian sausage (about 4 links) for the smoked sausage. Remove the casings, cut into ½-inch pieces and proceed with the recipe as directed.

Ramen Chili

MAKES 8 TO 10 SERVINGS

- 2 teaspoons vegetable oil
- 2 pounds ground beef
- 2 red onions, diced
- 1 red bell pepper, diced
- 6 tablespoons chili powder
- 4 teaspoons salt
- 2 teaspoons ground cumin
- ¼ teaspoon ground red pepper
- 4 cans (about 14 ounces each) diced tomatoes with basil, garlic and oregano
- 2 cans (about 15 ounces each) kidney beans, rinsed and drained
- 2 cups water
- 1 tablespoon packed brown sugar
- 1 package (3 ounces) ramen noodles, broken*
- Optional toppings: sour cream, shredded Cheddar cheese and thinly sliced green onions

**Use any flavor; discard seasoning packet.*

1 Heat oil in Dutch oven over medium-high heat. Add beef; brown 6 to 8 minutes, stirring to break up meat. Remove to large bowl with slotted spoon. Add onions and bell pepper to Dutch oven; cook and stir 6 minutes or until softened. Add chili powder, salt, cumin and ground red pepper; cook and stir 1 minute.

2 Return beef to Dutch oven; stir in tomatoes, beans, water and brown sugar. Bring to a boil. Reduce heat to medium-low; simmer 45 minutes, stirring occasionally. Stir in noodles; cook about 10 minutes or until noodles are tender. Serve with desired toppings.

Middle Eastern Turkey Meatballs with Couscous

MAKES 4 SERVINGS

- 1 cup chicken broth
- ⅔ cup uncooked whole wheat or plain couscous
- 1 teaspoon salt, divided
- 2 tablespoons olive oil, divided
- 1 cup finely chopped onion, divided
- 1 cup baby spinach
- 1 pound ground turkey
- 1 egg
- 1 tablespoon steak sauce
- ¾ teaspoon ground cinnamon
- ¾ teaspoon ground cumin
- ¼ teaspoon black pepper
- ½ cup water
- 2 tablespoons tomato paste

1 Bring broth to a boil in small saucepan over high heat; stir in couscous and ½ teaspoon salt. Cover and remove from heat; let stand 5 minutes.

2 Meanwhile, heat 1 tablespoon oil in large skillet over medium heat. Add ¾ cup onion; cook and stir 5 minutes or until tender. Stir into couscous with spinach. Set aside.

3 Combine turkey, egg, remaining ¼ cup onion, steak sauce, cinnamon, cumin, remaining ½ teaspoon salt and black pepper in medium bowl; mix well. Shape into 24 (1-inch) balls.

4 Heat remaining 1 tablespoon oil in same skillet over medium-high heat. Add meatballs; cook about 7 minutes or until no longer pink in center (165°F), turning frequently to brown on all sides. Remove meatballs to plate; keep warm.

5 Add water and tomato paste to skillet; whisk until blended. Bring to a boil; reduce heat to low. Add meatballs; cook until meatballs are coated with sauce, stirring gently. Serve meatballs over couscous mixture.

Peanut-Sauced Chicken and Green Beans

MAKES 4 SERVINGS

- ¼ cup hot water
- ¼ cup creamy peanut butter
- 2 tablespoons packed brown sugar
- 2 tablespoons soy sauce
- 1 clove garlic, minced
- ⅛ teaspoon black pepper
- 1 can (about 14 ounces) stewed tomatoes with onions, celery and green peppers
- 4 boneless skinless chicken breasts (6 to 8 ounces each)
- 1 teaspoon salt
- ½ cup plain dry bread crumbs
- 1 tablespoon vegetable oil
- 1 package (12 ounces) frozen cut green beans, thawed
- Hot cooked rice

1 Whisk hot water, peanut butter, brown sugar, soy sauce, garlic and pepper in medium bowl. Add tomatoes; break up large pieces with large spoon.

2 Season chicken with salt; coat with bread crumbs. Heat oil in large skillet over medium-high heat. Add chicken; cook 4 minutes or until golden brown on both sides.

3 Add green beans and tomato mixture to skillet. Reduce heat to medium-low; cover and simmer 15 minutes or until chicken is cooked through (165°F). Serve over rice.

Hurried Hearty Skillet Beef and Rice

MAKES 4 SERVINGS

- 1 cup uncooked rice
- ½ teaspoon ground turmeric (optional)
- 1 pound ground beef
- 1½ cups salsa
- ½ cup frozen corn
- 1 teaspoon beef bouillon granules
- 1 teaspoon ground cumin
- 1½ teaspoons sugar
- ½ teaspoon salt
- Sour cream (optional)

1. Cook rice according to package directions, adding turmeric, if desired.
2. Meanwhile, brown beef in large skillet over medium-high heat 6 to 8 minutes, stirring to break up meat. Stir in salsa, corn, bouillon granules, cumin, sugar and salt; bring to a boil. Reduce heat; cover and simmer 5 minutes or until thickened slightly.
3. Serve over rice and top with sour cream, if desired.

Chicken Tenders in Tomato Sauce

MAKES 4 SERVINGS

- 8 ounces chicken tenders
- 2 teaspoons Italian seasoning
- ½ teaspoon salt
- ¼ teaspoon black pepper
- 3 teaspoons olive oil, divided
- ¾ cup chopped yellow onion
- ¾ cup finely diced carrots
- ½ cup finely diced celery
- 1 can (about 14 ounces) diced tomatoes
- 1 clove garlic, minced

1. Sprinkle chicken with Italian seasoning, salt and pepper. Heat 2 teaspoons oil in large skillet over medium-high heat. Add chicken; cook 6 minutes or until chicken is cooked through (165°F) and no longer pink in center. Remove chicken from skillet; keep warm.
2. Reduce heat to medium; add remaining 1 teaspoon oil to skillet. Add onion, carrots and celery; cook and stir 5 minutes or until vegetables begin to soften.
3. Return chicken to skillet. Add tomatoes and garlic; mix well. Reduce heat to low; cover and simmer 10 minutes or until vegetables are heated through.

Balsamic Beef, Mushrooms and Onions

MAKES 4 SERVINGS

- 3 tablespoons olive oil, divided
- 2 large sweet onions, sliced
- ½ teaspoon salt, divided
- 4 teaspoons balsamic vinegar, divided
- 1 cup sliced mushrooms
- 1 boneless beef top sirloin (about 1 pound), cut into ½-inch-thick slices
- ¼ teaspoon dried thyme
- ¼ to ½ teaspoon black pepper

1 Heat 2 tablespoons oil large nonstick skillet over medium heat. Add onions; cook 15 minutes or until lightly browned, stirring occasionally.

2 Stir in 2 teaspoons oil and ¼ teaspoon salt. Add 3 teaspoons vinegar, 1 teaspoon at a time, stirring to scrape up browned bits. Reduce heat to medium-low. Add mushrooms; cook and stir 4 to 5 minutes or until mushrooms are tender. Transfer vegetables to medium bowl; keep warm.

3 Add remaining 1 teaspoon oil to skillet; heat over medium-high heat. Add beef; sprinkle with remaining ¼ teaspoon salt, thyme and pepper. Cook 4 to 6 minutes or until browned, stirring occasionally.

4 Remove from heat; drizzle with remaining 1 teaspoon vinegar. Stir in vegetables.

Chicken with Pomegranate-Orange Sauce

MAKES 4 SERVINGS

- 2 tablespoons soy sauce, divided
- 3 teaspoons cornstarch, divided
- 1 pound boneless skinless chicken breasts, cut into 1-inch cubes
- ½ cup pomegranate juice
- 1 to 2 tablespoons chili garlic sauce
- 1 teaspoon grated orange peel
- 1 teaspoon grated fresh ginger
- 1 tablespoon vegetable or peanut oil
- 2 stalks celery, cut diagonally into ¼-inch slices
- 1 red bell pepper, cut into 1-inch strips
- 2 oranges, peeled and sectioned
- 3 green onions, sliced
- Hot cooked rice

1 Stir 1 tablespoon soy sauce into 1 teaspoon cornstarch in medium bowl until smooth. Add chicken; stir to coat. Let stand 10 minutes.

2 Meanwhile, combine pomegranate juice, chili garlic sauce, remaining 1 tablespoon soy sauce, remaining 2 teaspoons cornstarch, orange peel and ginger in small bowl; stir until blended.

3 Heat oil in large nonstick skillet over medium-high heat. Add chicken; cook and stir 2 minutes. Add celery and bell pepper; stir-fry 3 minutes or until chicken is cooked through.

4 Stir pomegranate juice mixture; add to skillet. Bring to a boil over high heat. Reduce heat to medium-low; simmer 1 minute. Gently stir in orange sections; cook until heated through. Sprinkle with green onions and serve with rice.

Minestrone Skillet Dinner

MAKES 4 SERVINGS

- 2 slices bacon, chopped
- 1 tablespoon olive oil
- 2 cups coarsely shredded or chopped cabbage
- 1 zucchini, cut into ½-inch pieces
- 1 onion, chopped
- ¾ cup chopped carrots
- 1 stalk celery, chopped
- 1 clove garlic, minced
- 1 can (about 14 ounces) diced tomatoes
- 1 cup uncooked macaroni
- 1 cup water
- 1 can (about 15 ounces) Great Northern beans, rinsed and drained
- ½ teaspoon salt
- ½ teaspoon dried oregano
- ¼ teaspoon dried thyme
- ⅔ cup shredded Parmesan cheese

1 Preheat oven to 350°F. Cook and stir bacon in large ovenproof skillet over medium heat 5 minutes or until crisp, stirring occasionally. Transfer to paper towel-line plate with slotted spoon.

2 Heat oil in same skillet over medium-high heat. Add cabbage, zucchini, onion, carrots, celery and garlic; cook and stir 10 minutes or until cabbage is crisp-tender.

3 Stir in tomatoes, macaroni, water, beans, bacon, salt, oregano and thyme; simmer 5 minutes. Sprinkle with cheese.

4 Bake 15 minutes or until hot and bubbly and pasta is tender.

Tip

For a vegetarian dish, omit the bacon and increase the olive oil to 1½ tablespoons.

Casseroles & Sheet Pans

Mediterranean Sheet Pan Gnocchi

MAKES 4 TO 6 SERVINGS

- 1 package (16 to 17 ounces) shelf-stable gnocchi
- 2 medium zucchini, quartered lengthwise and cut crosswise into 1-inch pieces
- 2 medium red onions, halved and cut into ½-inch wedges
- 1 red bell pepper, cut into 1-inch pieces
- 1 pint grape or cherry tomatoes
- 2 cloves garlic, minced
- 1½ teaspoons salt
- 1 teaspoon dried oregano
- 1 teaspoon dried rosemary
- ½ teaspoon black pepper
- ¼ cup olive oil
- 2 cups baby arugula or shredded lacinato kale
- ½ cup crumbled feta cheese (optional)

1. Preheat oven to 425°F. Combine gnocchi, zucchini, onions, bell pepper and tomatoes on sheet pan.
2. Sprinkle with garlic, salt, oregano, rosemary and black pepper; drizzle with oil and toss to coat. Spread in single layer on sheet pan.
3. Bake 20 to 25 minutes or until tomatoes have burst, zucchini is tender and gnocchi is beginning to crisp, stirring halfway through cooking time. Stir in arugula; bake 1 to 2 minutes or just until arugula begins to wilt. Season with additional salt and black pepper; sprinkle with cheese, if desired.

Chicken and Tomato Rotini

MAKES 6 SERVINGS

- 1 package (16 ounces) uncooked rotini pasta
- 1 tablespoon olive oil
- 1 medium onion, chopped
- 2 cloves garlic, minced
- 1 can (6 ounces) tomato paste
- 1 can (about 28 ounces) diced tomatoes
- ½ cup whipping cream or half-and-half
- 1 teaspoon Italian seasoning
- ½ teaspoon salt
- 2 cups diced cooked chicken
- 2 cups (8 ounces) shredded mozzarella cheese
- ⅓ cup grated Parmesan cheese
- Minced fresh parsley or basil

1 Preheat oven to 350°F. Spray 13×9-inch baking dish with nonstick cooking spray. Cook pasta in large saucepan of salted boiling water according to package directions for al dente. Drain, reserving ½ cup cooking water.

2 Meanwhile, heat oil in large skillet over medium heat. Add onion; cook and stir 5 minutes or until softened. Add garlic; cook and stir 1 minute. Add tomato paste; cook and stir 2 minutes. Add tomatoes, cream, Italian seasoning and salt; cook and stir until well blended. Stir in chicken and reserved pasta cooking water. Add to pasta; mix well.

3 Spread half of pasta mixture in prepared baking dish; sprinkle with half of mozzarella cheese. Top with remaining pasta mixture and mozzarella cheese. Sprinkle with Parmesan cheese.

4 Cover and bake 25 minutes. Remove cover; sprinkle with remaining 1 cup mozzarella cheese and Parmesan cheese. Bake 5 to 10 minutes or until cheese is melted. Sprinkle with parsley.

Cajun Sausage and Shrimp Sheet Pan Dinner

MAKES 6 SERVINGS

- 2 pounds fingerling potatoes, cut in half
- 2 tablespoons olive oil, divided
- ½ teaspoon salt
- ¼ teaspoon plus ⅛ teaspoon black pepper, divided
- ¼ cup (½ stick) butter, melted
- 2 cloves garlic, minced
- 2 teaspoons Cajun seasoning
- 8 fresh ears of corn, cut in half *or* 1 package frozen corn on the cob (12 mini ears)
- 1 package (about 12 ounces) smoked turkey sausage, cut into ¼-inch coins
- 1 pound frozen shrimp, thawed according to package directions, peeled and deveined
- Juice of 1 lemon (about 3 tablespoons)
- ¼ cup minced fresh parsley

1. Preheat oven to 425°F. Combine potatoes, 1 tablespoon oil, salt and ⅛ teaspoon pepper in large bowl; toss to coat. Spread on sheet pan. Roast 20 minutes.
2. Whisk butter, remaining 1 tablespoon oil, ¼ teaspoon pepper, garlic and Cajun seasoning in small bowl until blended.
3. Stir potatoes; arrange corn and sausage on sheet pan around potatoes. Drizzle butter mixture all over vegetables and sausage. Bake 20 minutes or until potatoes are tender and corn is browned.
4. Add shrimp to sheet pan; bake 5 minutes or until shrimp are opaque. Drizzle with lemon juice; sprinkle with parsley.

Chili and Cheddar Baked Macaroni

MAKES 6 TO 8 SERVINGS

- 1 pound ground turkey
- 1 can (8 ounces) tomato sauce
- 1 small onion, diced
- 1 jalapeño pepper, seeded and minced
- 1 package (1¼ ounces) chili seasoning mix
- 1 cup water
- 1 package (16 ounces) uncooked elbow macaroni
- 2 cups (8 ounces) shredded sharp Cheddar cheese

1. Cook turkey in large skillet over medium-high heat 6 to 8 minutes or until no longer pink, stirring to break up meat. Drain fat. Stir in tomato sauce, onion, jalapeño and chili seasoning mix. Stir in water; bring to a boil. Reduce heat to low; simmer about 45 minutes or until chili is thick.
2. Preheat oven to 400°F. Spray 13×9-inch baking dish with nonstick cooking spray. Meanwhile, cook macaroni in large saucepan of salted boiling water according to package directions for al dente. Drain and return to saucepan.
3. Spread one third of macaroni in baking dish; top with one third of chili and one third of cheese. Repeat layers twice.
4. Bake 30 to 35 minutes or until edges begin to brown. Cool 5 to 10 minutes before serving.

Sheet Pan Gnocchi with Sausage, Mushrooms and Butternut Squash

MAKES 4 TO 6 SERVINGS

- 1 package (16 to 17 ounces) shelf-stable potato gnocchi
- 1 package (12 ounces) fully cooked Italian-style pork or chicken sausages, cut into ¾-inch slices
- 2½ cups cubed butternut squash (½-inch cubes, about 1 small squash)
- 2 medium red onions, halved and cut into ¾-inch wedges
- 8 ounces cremini and/or white mushrooms, cut into quarters
- 1½ teaspoons salt
- 1 teaspoon garlic powder
- ¾ teaspoon Italian seasoning
- ½ teaspoon black pepper
- 3 tablespoons olive oil

1. Preheat oven to 425°F. Combine gnocchi, sausage, squash, onions and mushrooms on sheet pan.
2. Sprinkle with salt, garlic powder, Italian seasoning and black pepper; drizzle with oil and toss to coat. Spread in single layer on sheet pan.
3. Bake 25 to 30 minutes or until vegetables are tender and gnocchi are beginning to brown, stirring halfway through cooking. Season with additional salt and pepper, if desired.

Ramen Reuben Noodle Bake

MAKES 8 SERVINGS

- 6 cups water
- 3 packages (3 ounces each) beef-flavored ramen noodles
- 2 cans (about 14 ounces each) shredded sauerkraut, undrained
- 1 pound thinly sliced deli corned beef, chopped
- ¼ cup (½ stick) butter, melted
- 1½ teaspoons caraway seeds, divided
- ½ cup Thousand Island dressing
- 8 slices (6 ounces) Swiss cheese

1 Preheat oven to 350°F. Spray 13×9-inch baking dish with nonstick cooking spray.

2 Bring water to a boil in large saucepan over high heat. Add noodles and ramen seasoning packets; return to a boil. Cook 2 to 3 minutes or until al dente; drain.

3 Combine noodles, sauerkraut with liquid, corned beef, butter and 1 teaspoon caraway seeds in large bowl; toss to coat. Spread in prepared baking dish.

4 Cover and bake 20 minutes. Drizzle dressing evenly over top. Arrange cheese on top; sprinkle with remaining ½ teaspoon caraway seeds. Bake, uncovered, 13 to 15 minutes or until cheese is melted and casserole is bubbly.

Sheet Pan Mediterranean Chicken

MAKES 6 SERVINGS

- ¼ cup olive oil
- 4 cloves garlic, thinly sliced
- 1 tablespoon red wine vinegar
- 2 teaspoons salt
- 1½ teaspoons smoked paprika
- 1 teaspoon dried oregano
- ½ teaspoon black pepper
- 6 boneless skinless chicken thighs (about 2 pounds)
- 2 cans (about 15 ounces each) chickpeas, rinsed and drained
- 3 pints grape tomatoes
- ½ cup pitted Kalamata olives, cut into halves
- ¾ cup crumbled feta cheese
- ½ cup chopped fresh parsley
- Hot cooked orzo (optional)

1. Preheat oven to 425°F. Line sheet pan with foil or spray with nonstick cooking spray.
2. Whisk oil, garlic, vinegar, salt, smoked paprika, oregano and pepper in large bowl until well blended. Add chicken, chickpeas, tomatoes and olives; stir to coat well. Spread mixture on prepared baking sheet. (Baking sheet will be very full.)
3. Bake 18 to 20 minutes or until chicken is cooked through (165°F) and tomatoes are beginning to burst. *Turn oven to broil;* broil 2 to 3 minutes or until chicken begins to brown.
4. Sprinkle with cheese and parsley. Serve with orzo, if desired.

Chicken and Rice Casserole

MAKES 4 SERVINGS

- 1 package boil-in-bag rice *or* 1 cup uncooked instant rice
- 1 tablespoon butter
- 1 pound boneless skinless chicken breasts, cut into bite-size pieces
- 3 tablespoons lemon juice
- ½ teaspoon salt
- ⅛ teaspoon black pepper
- 1 can (10½ ounces) cream of chicken soup
- ½ cup (2 ounces) shredded sharp Cheddar cheese
- Sliced green onions

1. Preheat oven to 350°F. Cook rice according to package directions.
2. Meanwhile, melt butter in large skillet over medium heat. Add chicken; cook and stir 5 to 6 minutes or until no longer pink in center. Add rice, lemon juice, salt and pepper. Stir in soup until blended. Transfer mixture to 9-inch square baking dish. Sprinkle cheese evenly over top.
3. Bake 20 minutes or until heated through and cheese is melted. Sprinkle with green onions.

Sheet Pan Chicken and Sausage Supper

MAKES ABOUT 6 SERVINGS

- ⅓ cup olive oil
- 2 tablespoons balsamic vinegar
- 1 teaspoon salt
- 1 teaspoon garlic powder
- ½ teaspoon black pepper
- ¼ teaspoon red pepper flakes
- 3 pounds bone-in chicken thighs and drumsticks
- 1 pound uncooked sweet Italian sausage (4 to 5 links), cut diagonally into 2-inch pieces
- 6 to 8 small red onions (about 1½ pounds), each cut into 6 wedges
- 3½ cups broccoli florets

1 Preheat oven to 425°F. Line sheet pan with foil, if desired.

2 Whisk oil, vinegar, salt, garlic powder, black pepper and red pepper flakes in small bowl until well blended. Combine chicken, sausage and onions on prepared sheet pan. Drizzle with oil mixture; toss until well coated. Spread meat and onions in single layer; arrange chicken thighs skin side up.

3 Bake 30 minutes. Add broccoli to baking sheet; stir to coat broccoli with pan juices and turn sausage. Bake 30 minutes or until broccoli is beginning to brown and chicken is cooked through (165°F).

Stroganoff Casserole

MAKES 8 SERVINGS

- 1 package (16 ounces) uncooked egg noodles
- 2 cans (10½ ounces each) cream of mushroom soup
- 1 container (8 ounces) sour cream
- ½ cup milk
- 1 pound ground beef
- 2 cans (6 ounces each) sliced mushrooms, undrained
- 1 package (8 ounces) cream cheese, softened
- 1 package (1 ounce) dry gravy mix

1 Preheat oven to 350°F. Cook noodles in large saucepan of salted boiling water according to package directions for al dente. Drain and return to saucepan; stir in soups, sour cream and milk.

2 Meanwhile, brown beef in large skillet over medium-high heat 6 to 8 minutes, stirring to break up meat. Drain fat. Add mushrooms, cream cheese and gravy mix to skillet; cook and stir until well blended. Add beef mixture to noodles; stir gently to coat. Spread in 13×9-inch baking dish.

3 Bake 30 minutes or until heated through.

Cauliflower, Sausage and Gouda Sheet Pan

MAKES 6 SERVINGS

- 1 package (16 ounces) mushrooms, trimmed and halved
- 3 tablespoons olive oil, divided
- 1 teaspoon salt, divided
- 1 head cauliflower, separated into florets and thinly sliced
- ¼ teaspoon chipotle chili powder
- 1 package (about 13 ounces) smoked sausage, cut into ¼-inch slices
- 2 tablespoons peach or apricot preserves
- 1 tablespoon Dijon mustard
- ½ red onion, thinly sliced
- 6 ounces Gouda cheese, cubed

1. Preheat oven to 400°F.
2. Place mushrooms in medium bowl. Drizzle with 1 tablespoon oil and sprinkle with ½ teaspoon salt; toss to coat. Spread on sheet pan.
3. Combine cauliflower, remaining 2 tablespoons oil, ½ teaspoon salt and chipotle chili powder in same bowl; toss to coat. Spread on sheet pan with mushrooms.
4. Combine sausage, preserves and mustard in same bowl; stir until well coated. Arrange sausage over vegetables; top with onion.
5. Bake 30 minutes. Remove from oven; sprinkle cheese cubes over top. Bake 5 minutes or until cheese is melted and cauliflower is tender.

Fiesta Beef Enchiladas

MAKES 6 SERVINGS

- 1 pound ground beef
- ½ cup sliced green onions
- 2 teaspoons minced garlic
- 1½ cups chopped tomatoes, divided
- 1 cup cooked white or brown rice
- 1 cup (4 ounces) shredded Mexican cheese blend or Cheddar cheese, divided
- ¾ cup frozen corn
- ½ cup salsa or picante sauce
- 12 (6- to 7-inch) corn tortillas
- 1 can (10 ounces) enchilada sauce
- 1 cup shredded romaine lettuce

1. Preheat oven to 375°F. Spray 13×9-inch baking dish with nonstick cooking spray.
2. Brown beef in large skillet over medium-high heat 6 to 8 minutes, stirring to break up meat. Drain fat. Add green onions and garlic; cook and stir 2 minutes. Remove from heat; stir in 1 cup tomatoes, rice, ½ cup cheese, corn and salsa.
3. Spoon beef mixture down center of tortillas. Roll up; place seam side down in prepared baking dish. Spoon enchilada sauce evenly over enchiladas.
4. Cover and bake 20 minutes or until heated through. Sprinkle with remaining ½ cup cheese; bake 5 minutes or until cheese is melted. Serve with lettuce and remaining ½ cup tomatoes.

Sandwiches & Handhelds

Turkey Sloppy Joes

MAKES 8 SERVINGS

- 1 cup ketchup
- 2 tablespoons packed brown sugar
- 2 tablespoons Worcestershire sauce
- 2 tablespoons yellow mustard
- 2 tablespoons cider vinegar
- 1 tablespoon vegetable oil
- 2 pounds ground turkey
- 1 medium onion, chopped
- 1 red bell pepper, chopped
- 1 clove garlic, minced
- 2 teaspoons chili powder
- ½ teaspoon salt
- ½ teaspoon ground cumin
- ¼ teaspoon black pepper
- 8 hamburger buns

1. Combine ketchup, brown sugar, Worcestershire sauce, mustard and vinegar in medium bowl.
2. Heat oil in large skillet over medium-high heat. Add turkey, onion, bell pepper and garlic; cook and stir 10 minutes or until turkey is no longer pink, stirring to break up meat. Add chili powder, salt, cumin and black pepper; cook and stir 1 minute.
3. Add ketchup mixture to skillet; mix well. Cook 10 minutes, stirring occasionally. Serve on buns.

Cheesy Mushroom Melt

MAKES 4 SERVINGS

- 4 French rolls
- 4 slices (1 ounce each) Swiss cheese
- 4 slices (1 ounce each) Cheddar cheese
- 4 slices (1 ounce each) provolone cheese
- 2 cups sliced mushrooms
- 1 avocado, thinly sliced
- 1 cup thinly sliced iceberg lettuce
- ½ cup thinly sliced yellow or white onion
- 2 plum tomatoes, thinly sliced
- 2 dill pickles, thinly sliced lengthwise
- Optional toppings: mayonnaise, mustard, vinaigrette, sliced banana peppers and/or giardiniera

1 Preheat oven to 400°F. Line baking sheet with foil. Split sides and long ends of rolls, leaving one long end attached. Place rolls cut sides down on prepared baking sheet. Bake 5 minutes.

2 Remove baking sheet from oven; turn rolls over. For each sandwich, cut one slice of each cheese in half diagonally; arrange cheese halves on each half of roll, overlapping to fit. Top each bottom half of roll with ½ cup mushrooms.

3 Bake 5 to 7 minutes until cheese is melted and bread is toasted.

4 Layer avocado, lettuce, onion, tomatoes, pickles and desired toppings over mushrooms. Close sandwiches and press gently; cut in half to serve.

Mediterranean Roasted Vegetable Wraps

MAKES 4 SERVINGS

- 1 head cauliflower, cut into 1-inch florets
- 4 tablespoons olive oil, divided
- 2 teaspoons ras el hanout, 7-spice blend, shawarma blend or za'atar
- 1 teaspoon salt, divided
- 1 zucchini, quartered lengthwise and cut into ¼-inch pieces
- 1 yellow squash, quartered lengthwise and cut into ¼-inch pieces
- ½ red onion, thinly sliced
- ¼ cup red pepper sauce (avjar)
- 4 large thin pitas, lavash or tortillas (10 inches)
- 4 ounces feta cheese, crumbled
- 1 cup drained canned chickpeas
- ¼ cup diced tomatoes
- ¼ cup minced fresh parsley
- ¼ cup diced cucumber (optional)
- 2 teaspoons vegetable oil

1 Preheat oven to 400°F. Combine cauliflower, 2 tablespoons olive oil, ras el hanout and ½ teaspoon salt in large bowl; toss to coat. Spread on half of sheet pan. Combine zucchini, yellow squash, onion, remaining 2 tablespoons olive oil and ½ teaspoon salt in same bowl; toss to coat. Spread on other side of sheet pan. Roast 25 minutes or until vegetables are browned and tender, stirring once. Remove from oven; cool slightly.

2 Spread 1 tablespoon red pepper sauce on one pita. Top with one fourth of vegetables, feta, chickpeas, tomatoes, parsley and cucumber, if desired. Fold two sides over filling; roll up into burrito shape. Repeat with remaining ingredients.

3 Heat 1 teaspoon vegetable oil in large skillet over medium-high heat. Add two wraps, seam sides down; cook 1 minute or until browned. Turn and cook other side until browned. Repeat with remaining vegetable oil and wraps. Cut in half to serve.

Chicken Fajita Roll-Ups

MAKES 4 SERVINGS

- 1 cup ranch dressing
- 1 teaspoon chili powder
- 2 tablespoons vegetable oil, divided
- 2 teaspoons fajita seasoning mix
- 2 teaspoons lime juice
- ½ teaspoon chipotle chili powder
- ¼ teaspoon salt
- 4 boneless skinless chicken breasts (6 to 8 ounces each)
- 4 fajita-size flour tortillas (8 to 9 inches)
- 1 cup (4 ounces) shredded Cheddar cheese
- 1 cup (4 ounces) shredded Monterey Jack cheese
- 3 cups shredded lettuce
- 1 cup pico de gallo

1 Combine ranch dressing and chili powder in small bowl; mix well. Refrigerate until ready to serve.

2 Combine 1 tablespoon oil, fajita seasoning mix, lime juice, chipotle chili powder and salt in small bowl; mix well. Coat both sides of chicken with spice mixture.

3 Heat remaining 1 tablespoon oil in large nonstick skillet or grill pan over medium-high heat. Add chicken; cook 6 minutes per side or until cooked through (165°F). Remove to plate; let stand 5 minutes before slicing. Cut chicken breasts in half lengthwise, then cut crosswise into ½-inch strips.

4 Wipe out skillet with paper towel. Place one tortilla in skillet; sprinkle with ¼ cup Cheddar and ¼ cup Monterey Jack. Heat over medium heat until cheeses are melted. Remove tortilla to clean work surface or cutting board.

5 Sprinkle ¾ cup shredded lettuce down center of tortilla; top with ¼ cup pico de gallo and one fourth of chicken. Fold bottom of tortilla up over filling, then fold in sides and roll up. Cut in half diagonally. Repeat with remaining tortillas, cheese and fillings. Serve with ranch dipping sauce.

Grilled Prosciutto, Brie and Fig Sandwiches

MAKES 2 SANDWICHES

¼ cup fig preserves

4 slices (½ to ¾ inch thick) Italian or country bread

Black pepper

4 to 6 ounces Brie cheese, cut into ¼-inch-thick slices

2 slices prosciutto (about half of 3-ounce package)

¼ cup baby arugula

1½ tablespoons butter

1 Spread preserves over two bread slices. Sprinkle pepper generously over preserves. Top with Brie, prosciutto, arugula and remaining bread slices.

2 Heat medium skillet over medium heat 5 minutes. Add 1 tablespoon butter; swirl to melt and coat bottom of skillet. Add sandwiches to skillet; cook over medium-low heat about 5 minutes or until bottoms of sandwiches are golden brown.

3 Turn sandwiches and add remaining ½ tablespoon butter to skillet. Tilt pan to melt butter and move sandwiches so butter flows underneath. Cover with foil; cook about 5 minutes or until cheese is melted and bread is golden brown.

Grilled Buffalo Chicken Wraps

MAKES 4 SERVINGS

- 4 boneless skinless chicken breasts (6 to 8 ounces each)
- ¼ cup plus 2 tablespoons buffalo wing sauce, divided
- 2 cups broccoli slaw mix
- 1 tablespoon blue cheese dressing
- 4 (8-inch) whole wheat tortillas, warmed

1. Place chicken in large bowl. Add ¼ cup buffalo sauce; turn to coat chicken with sauce. Let stand 15 minutes.
2. Meanwhile, prepare grill for direct cooking over medium-high heat. Grill chicken 5 to 6 minutes per side or until no longer pink in center (165°F). Cut chicken into ½-inch slices when cool enough to handle. Combine chicken and remaining 2 tablespoons buffalo sauce in medium bowl; toss to coat.
3. Combine broccoli slaw and blue cheese dressing in another medium bowl; mix well.
4. Layer chicken and broccoli slaw over center of third of each tortilla. Roll up tortilla to enclose filling. Cut in half diagonally.

Mushroom, Olive and Chicken Pizza

MAKES 4 SERVINGS

- 1 package (8 ounces) refrigerated crescent rolls
- 2 tablespoons vegetable oil
- 1 pound boneless skinless chicken breasts, cut into 1-inch pieces
- 1 green bell pepper, sliced into rings
- 1 large onion, chopped
- 8 ounces sliced mushrooms
- ½ cup pitted black olives, sliced
- ½ cup pizza sauce
- 1 teaspoon garlic salt
- 1 teaspoon dried oregano
- ¼ cup grated Parmesan cheese
- 1½ cups (6 ounces) shredded mozzarella cheese

1. Preheat oven to 425°F.
2. Separate dough into eight triangles. Press triangles into greased 12-inch pizza pan, covering bottom of pan completely. Seal seams.
3. Heat oil in large skillet over medium-high heat. Add chicken, pepper, onion, mushrooms and olives; cook and stir 5 minutes or until chicken is no longer pink in center.
4. Spread pizza sauce over dough. Spoon chicken mixture over top. Sprinkle with garlic salt, oregano and Parmesan cheese. Top with mozzarella cheese.
5. Bake 20 minutes or until crust is golden brown. Cut into wedges to serve.

Speedy Tacos

MAKES 4 SERVINGS

- 8 ounces ground beef
- 1 cup chopped onion, divided
- 2 cloves garlic, minced
- ⅔ cup tomato sauce
- 2 tablespoons taco seasoning mix
- 12 hard taco shells
- ½ cup (4 ounces) shredded Cheddar cheese
- 1 cup shredded lettuce
- ⅔ cup chopped tomato

1. Heat medium skillet over medium heat. Add beef, ½ cup onion and garlic; cook and stir 5 minutes or until beef is browned, stirring to break up meat. Add tomato sauce and taco seasoning mix; cook and stir 5 minutes.
2. Warm taco shells in oven according to package directions.
3. Fill taco shells with beef mixture, cheese, lettuce, tomato and remaining ½ cup onion.

Turkey and Spinach Panini with Basil-Dijon Aïoli

MAKES 4 SERVINGS

- 3 tablespoons mayonnaise
- 1 tablespoon coarse-grain Dijon mustard
- 1 teaspoon dried basil
- 2 cloves garlic, minced
- 1 loaf (12 to 16 ounces) whole-grain Italian bread, cut in half lengthwise
- ¾ cup (3 ounces) shredded mozzarella cheese
- 1 medium tomato, thinly sliced
- ½ cup thinly sliced red onion
- 4 ounces thinly sliced oven-roasted turkey
- 2 ounces fresh baby spinach leaves

1. For aïoli, combine mayonnaise, mustard, basil and garlic in small bowl.
2. Remove soft inside portion of bread, leaving about ½-inch-thick shell. (Reserve bread pieces for another use, such as for bread crumbs or croutons.)
3. Sprinkle cheese on bottom half of bread. Top with tomato, onion, turkey and spinach. Spread aïoli on top portion of bread. Close sandwich; press lightly.
4. Spray large skillet with nonstick cooking spray; heat over medium heat. Place sandwich in skillet. Weigh down with a dinner plate to compress sandwiches. Cook about 5 minutes or until bread is golden and cheese is melted. Cut into four pieces.

Tomatillo Pork Tacos

MAKES 4 SERVINGS

- 2 teaspoons vegetable oil
- 1 pound pork tenderloin, cut into ½-inch chunks
- 1 teaspoon ground cumin
- 1 teaspoon chili powder
- ½ teaspoon salt
- ½ cup chopped onion
- 3 cloves garlic, minced
- ¾ cup tomatillo salsa, divided
- 8 (6-inch) flour tortillas, warmed
- 1 cup diced ripe tomato
- 1 cup shredded romaine lettuce
- ½ cup (2 ounces) shredded Mexican cheese blend or crumbled queso fresco

1. Heat oil in large skillet over medium heat. Add pork, cumin, chili powder and salt; stir until pork is coated with spices. Add onion and garlic; cook and stir 5 minutes or until onion is softened. Add ½ cup salsa; simmer about 4 minutes or until pork is cooked through (145°F).
2. Serve pork mixture in tortillas topped with tomato, lettuce, cheese and remaining ¼ cup salsa.

Chicken Pesto Pizzas with Spinach and Tomatoes >

MAKES 4 SERVINGS

- 1 package (10 ounces) prepared whole wheat pizza crust
- ⅓ cup pesto sauce
- 1 cup shredded or chopped cooked chicken
- 1 plum tomato, thinly sliced
- ½ cup baby spinach, coarsely chopped
- ¾ cup (3 ounces) shredded mozzarella cheese

1. Preheat oven to 450°F.
2. Place pizza crust on pizza pan or baking sheet. Spread pesto evenly over crust; layer with chicken, tomato and spinach. Sprinkle with cheese.
3. Bake 10 to 12 minutes or until cheese is melted and edge of crust is browned.

Prosciutto, Asparagus and Chicken Pizza

MAKES 4 SERVINGS

- 1 package (10 ounces) prepared whole wheat pizza crust
- ½ cup pizza sauce
- 4 asparagus spears, cut into 1-inch pieces
- ½ cup chopped prosciutto
- ½ cup chopped red onion
- 1 cup shredded cooked chicken
- ¾ cup (3 ounces) shredded mozzarella cheese

1. Preheat oven to 450°F.
2. Place pizza crust on baking sheet. Spread pizza sauce over crust and layer with asparagus, prosciutto, onion and chicken. Sprinkle with cheese.
3. Bake 10 to 12 minutes or until cheese is melted and edge of crust is browned.

Southwestern BLT >

MAKES 2 SERVINGS

- 6 slices thick-cut applewood smoked bacon
- ¼ cup mayonnaise
- 1 teaspoon lime juice
- ¼ teaspoon ground chipotle pepper
- ¼ teaspoon ground cumin
- 1 large ripe tomato
- 2 pretzel rolls, split and toasted
- ½ cup shredded lettuce

1 Cook bacon in large skillet over medium heat until crisp; drain on paper towel-lined plate.

2 Combine mayonnaise, lime juice, chipotle pepper and cumin in small bowl.

3 Cut tomato into four thick slices. Spread cut sides of rolls with mayonnaise mixture; layer with lettuce, tomato and bacon. Close sandwiches.

Open-Faced Garden Ranch Tuna Salad Sandwiches

MAKES 4 SERVINGS

- 2 cans (5 ounces each) chunk white tuna in water, drained
- 3 tablespoons ranch dressing
- ¼ cup diced peeled cucumber
- ¼ cup diced celery
- ¼ cup shredded carrot
- 1 small tomato, cut into 8 thin slices
- 2 English muffins, split and toasted
- 2 teaspoons fresh chopped dill

1 Combine tuna, dressing, cucumber, celery and carrot in medium bowl.

2 Place two tomato slices on each English muffin half. Top each evenly with tuna mixture and dill.

Pasta & Grains

Balsamic Tomato Penne

MAKES 4 TO 6 SERVINGS

- 1 package (16 ounces) uncooked penne pasta
- 6 tablespoons olive oil, divided
- ½ red onion, cut into ⅛-inch slices
- ¼ cup balsamic vinegar
- 4 plum tomatoes, cut into ½-inch dice (2½ cups)
- 6 cloves roasted garlic*
- 1 teaspoon salt
- 1 package (5 ounces) fresh spinach, stemmed
- Shredded Parmesan cheese

**To roast garlic, cut top off one head of garlic to expose top of cloves. Place on piece of foil; drizzle with 1 teaspoon olive oil and season lightly with salt. Wrap tightly in foil. Roast at 400°F 35 to 40 minutes or until soft. Squeeze garlic from skins when cool enough to handle.*

1 Cook pasta in large saucepan of salted boiling water according to package directions for al dente. Drain and place in large serving bowl; stir in 2 tablespoons oil.

2 Meanwhile, heat remaining ¼ cup oil in large skillet over medium-high heat. Add onion; cook and stir 5 minutes or until softened. Reduce heat to medium. Add vinegar; cook 3 minutes or until slightly reduced.

3 Add tomatoes, roasted garlic and salt; cook and stir 1 minute. Add spinach; cook 1 minute or just until wilted. Pour sauce over pasta; stir to coat. Serve with cheese.

Alfredo Bolognese Spaghetti Skillet

MAKES 6 TO 8 SERVINGS

- 1 package (16 ounces) uncooked spaghetti
- 1 jar (about 15 ounces) Alfredo sauce
- 1 pound ground beef or ground meat substitute
- 1 onion, chopped
- 2 cloves garlic, minced
- 1 teaspoon Italian seasoning
- ½ teaspoon salt
- ¼ teaspoon black pepper
- 1 jar (about 24 ounces) marinara sauce
- 1 cup (4 ounces) shredded mozzarella cheese
- Red pepper flakes (optional)

1 Preheat oven to 350°F. Cook spaghetti in large saucepan of salted boiling water according to package directions for al dente. Drain and return to saucepan; stir in Alfredo sauce. Cover and keep warm.

2 Meanwhile, cook beef, onion and garlic in large ovenproof skillet over medium-high heat about 10 minutes or until beef is no longer pink, stirring to break up meat. Stir in Italian seasoning, salt and black pepper. Reduce heat to medium-low. Stir in marinara sauce; cook 10 minutes, stirring frequently.

3 Transfer sauce to large bowl. Spread spaghetti mixture in same skillet; top with meat sauce and sprinkle with cheese. Bake 20 minutes or until pasta is heated through and cheese is melted. Sprinkle with red pepper flakes, if desired.

Lentils with Pasta

MAKES 6 TO 8 SERVINGS

- 1 cup dried lentils
- 1 cup dried split peas
- 1 tablespoon olive oil
- 1 onion, chopped
- 2 tablespoons tomato paste
- 2 cloves garlic, minced
- 1 teaspoon salt
- ¼ teaspoon black pepper
- 1 can (about 14 ounces) diced tomatoes
- 3 cups water
- 12 ounces uncooked short pasta (small shells, elbow macaroni, ditalini or similar)
- Grated Romano or Parmesan cheese (optional)

1. Place lentils and split peas in medium bowl; cover with water. Let stand at least 10 minutes.
2. Heat oil in large saucepan or Dutch oven over medium heat. Add onion; cook and stir 5 minutes or until onion is lightly browned. Add tomato paste, garlic, salt and pepper; cook and stir 1 minute. Add tomatoes and 3 cups water; bring to a boil.
3. Drain lentils and split peas and add to saucepan. Reduce heat to medium-low; cover and simmer about 40 minutes or until lentils and split peas are tender.
4. Meanwhile, cook pasta in large saucepan of salted boiling water according to package directions for al dente. Drain and add to lentil mixture; mix well. Serve with cheese, if desired.

French Onion Pasta

MAKES 4 TO 6 SERVINGS

- ¼ cup (½ stick) butter
- 1½ pounds yellow onions (3 medium), thinly sliced
- ¾ teaspoon salt, divided
- ¼ teaspoon black pepper
- 2 cups cubed French or Italian bread
- 2 tablespoons olive oil
- ⅓ cup sherry or white wine
- 12 ounces uncooked campanelle pasta or other short pasta shape
- 4 cups mushroom or vegetable broth
- 6 fresh thyme sprigs
- ¼ cup whipping cream
- 1½ cups (6 ounces) shredded Gruyère or Swiss cheese

1 Melt butter in large (12-inch) cast iron skillet over medium-low heat; add onions. Cook about 45 minutes or until onions are dark golden brown, stirring frequently and adding water by tablespoons if onions appear dry. Stir in ¼ teaspoon salt and black pepper.

2 Meanwhile, preheat oven to 350°F. Toss bread cubes and oil in large bowl until well coated. Spread on small baking sheet. Bake 20 minutes or until bread cubes are toasted, stirring once.

3 Increase heat to medium-high. Add sherry to skillet, stirring to scrape up browned bits. Add pasta, broth, thyme sprigs and remaining ½ teaspoon salt; mix well. Bring to a boil; cook 10 minutes or until broth is absorbed and pasta is tender, stirring frequently. Remove from heat; remove thyme springs. Stir in cream. Top with cheese; cover and let stand until cheese is melted, or broil until melted and browned. Top with toasted bread cubes.

Roasted Garlic Mac and Cheese

MAKES 8 TO 10 SERVINGS

- 1 head garlic
- 1 tablespoon olive oil
- 6 tablespoons butter, divided
- 1 cup panko bread crumbs
- 1¼ teaspoons salt, divided
- 1 package (16 ounces) uncooked cellentani pasta or elbow macaroni
- ¼ cup all-purpose flour
- ½ teaspoon black pepper
- 2 cups whole milk
- ¾ cup Irish stout*
- 2 cups (8 ounces) shredded sharp Cheddar cheese
- 2 cups (8 ounces) shredded Dubliner or white Cheddar cheese

***Or substitute additional milk.**

1 Preheat oven to 375°F. Spray 4-quart baking dish with nonstick cooking spray.

2 Place garlic on 10-inch piece of foil; drizzle with oil and crimp shut. Place on small baking sheet; bake 30 to 40 minutes or until tender. Cool 15 minutes; squeeze cloves into small bowl. Mash into smooth paste.*

3 Melt 2 tablespoons butter in small saucepan over medium heat. Stir in panko and ¼ teaspoon salt until well blended.

4 Cook pasta in large saucepan of salted boiling water according to package directions for al dente. Drain and return to saucepan; keep warm.

5 Meanwhile, melt remaining 4 tablespoons butter in large saucepan over medium heat. Add flour; cook and stir until lightly browned. Stir in roasted garlic, remaining 1 teaspoon salt and pepper. Slowly whisk in milk and stout; cook until thickened, whisking constantly. Remove from heat; whisk in cheeses, ½ cup at a time, until melted. Add cheese mixture to pasta; stir to coat. Spoon into prepared baking dish; sprinkle with panko mixture.

6 Bake 40 minutes or until bubbly and topping is golden brown. Let stand 10 minutes before serving.

**Garlic can be roasted ahead of time; store in refrigerator until ready to use.*

Cajun Red Beans and Rice

MAKES 4 SERVINGS

- 1 cup uncooked white rice
- 1 can (about 15 ounces) red beans, rinsed and drained
- ½ cup cubed ham
- 1½ cups water
- 1 can (about 14 ounces) chicken broth
- ¼ cup tomato paste
- 1 teaspoon Cajun seasoning
- ½ teaspoon salt
- ⅛ teaspoon ground red pepper
- 1 bay leaf
- 1 tablespoon olive oil
- 1 green bell pepper, chopped
- ¾ cup chopped onion
- ¾ cup sliced celery
- Hot pepper sauce (optional)

1 Combine rice, beans, ham, water, broth, tomato paste, Cajun seasoning, salt, red pepper and bay leaf in large saucepan. Bring to a boil over medium-high heat. Reduce heat to low; cover and simmer 15 minutes.

2 Meanwhile, heat oil in medium skillet over medium heat until hot. Add bell pepper, onion and celery; cook and stir 5 minutes or until vegetables are softened. Stir into rice mixture; cover and simmer 10 minutes or until rice is tender. Remove and discard bay leaf. Serve with hot pepper sauce.

Classic Fettuccine Alfredo

MAKES 4 SERVINGS

12 ounces uncooked fettuccine
⅔ cup whipping cream
6 tablespoons butter
½ teaspoon salt
Generous dash white pepper
Generous dash ground nutmeg
1 cup grated Parmesan cheese
2 tablespoons chopped fresh parsley

1 Cook pasta in large saucepan of salted boiling water according to package directions for al dente. Drain and return to saucepan; keep warm.

2 Meanwhile, heat cream and butter in large heavy skillet over medium-low heat until butter melts and mixture bubbles, stirring frequently. Cook and stir 2 minutes. Stir in salt, pepper and nutmeg. Remove from heat; gradually stir in cheese until well blended and smooth. Return to low heat, if necessary; do not let sauce bubble or cheese will become lumpy and tough.

3 Pour sauce over pasta; cook and stir over low heat 2 to 3 minutes or until sauce is thickened and pasta is evenly coated. Sprinkle with parsley.

Lentils, Pepper and Feta Rice

MAKES 6 SERVINGS

- ½ cup sun-dried tomatoes, packed in oil
- 1 tablespoon olive oil
- 6 ounces ham, finely chopped
- 2 cups chopped green bell peppers
- 1 cup chopped onion
- 6 cups water
- 8 ounces dried brown lentils, rinsed and sorted
- 1 tablespoon Italian seasoning
- ½ teaspoon salt
- 2 cups uncooked instant brown rice
- 4 ounces crumbled feta cheese, plain or sun-dried tomato and basil flavor

1. Drain tomatoes, reserving 1 teaspoon oil; chop tomatoes.
2. Heat olive oil in Dutch oven over medium-high heat. Add ham; cook and stir 3 minutes or until lightly browned. Transfer to small bowl; set aside.
3. Add reserved tomato oil to Dutch oven; heat over medium heat. Add bell peppers, onion and tomatoes; cook and stir 5 minutes or until onion is tender.
4. Add water to Dutch oven; bring to a boil over high heat. Add lentils, Italian seasoning and salt; return to a boil. Reduce heat; cover and simmer 30 minutes or until lentils are tender. Remove from heat; stir in ham. Cover and let stand 15 minutes.
5. Meanwhile, cook rice according to package directions. Serve lentil mixture over rice; sprinkle with feta.

Mediterranean Mac and Cheese

MAKES 4 TO 6 SERVINGS

- 8 ounces uncooked elbow macaroni or other small pasta shape
- 1 tablespoon olive oil
- 1 red bell pepper, thinly sliced
- 1 bunch (about ¾ pound) asparagus, cut into 1-inch pieces
- 4 tablespoons butter, divided
- ¼ cup all-purpose flour
- 1¾ cups milk
- 1 teaspoon minced fresh thyme
- Salt and black pepper
- 1 cup (4 ounces) shredded mozzarella cheese
- 1 cup chopped cooked chicken
- 4 ounces garlic and herb flavored goat cheese
- ¼ cup plain dry bread crumbs

1 Preheat oven to 350°F. Cook macaroni in large saucepan of salted boiling water 2 minutes less than package directs for al dente. Drain and rinse under cold water to stop cooking.

2 Meanwhile, heat oil in medium skillet over medium-high heat. Add bell pepper; cook and stir 3 minutes. Add asparagus; cook and stir 3 minutes or until crisp-tender. Remove from heat.

3 Melt 3 tablespoons butter in large saucepan or deep skillet over medium heat until bubbly. Whisk in flour until smooth paste forms; cook and stir 2 minutes without browning. Gradually whisk in milk; cook 6 to 8 minutes, whisking constantly until mixture begins to bubble and thickens slightly. Add thyme and season with salt and black pepper. Remove from heat.

4 Stir in mozzarella cheese until melted. Add pasta, bell pepper, asparagus and chicken to cheese sauce. Crumble goat cheese into mixture; spread in 2-quart baking dish. Top with bread crumbs and dot with remaining 1 tablespoon butter.

5 Bake 25 to 30 minutes or until lightly browned and bubbly.

White Beans and Pasta Puttanesca

MAKES 4 SERVINGS

- 8 ounces uncooked spaghetti
- 2 tablespoons olive oil
- 2 cups diced zucchini (¼-inch pieces)
- 1 can (about 15 ounces) cannellini beans, rinsed and drained
- 1 can (about 14 ounces) diced tomatoes with basil, garlic and oregano
- ½ cup water
- 2 tablespoons tomato paste
- 1 tablespoon capers, rinsed and drained
- ½ teaspoon salt
- ⅛ teaspoon red pepper flakes
- 6 tablespoons grated Parmesan cheese
- ¼ cup chopped fresh parsley

1. Cook spaghetti in large saucepan of salted boiling water according to package directions for al dente. Drain and return to saucepan; keep warm.
2. Heat oil in large skillet over medium-high heat. Add zucchini; cook 5 minutes or until browned in spots, stirring occasionally. Stir in beans, tomatoes, water, tomato paste, capers, salt and red pepper flakes; cover and bring to a simmer. Reduce heat to low; cook 7 minutes or until zucchini is tender and sauce is slightly thickened.
3. Serve sauce over spaghetti; top with cheese and parsley.

Pasta Paprikash

MAKES 4 TO 6 SERVINGS

- 8 ounces uncooked long pasta (linguine, fettuccine or spaghetti)
- 2 tablespoons olive oil
- 2 red bell peppers, cut into short thin strips
- 1 medium onion, thinly sliced
- 1 clove garlic, minced
- 2 tablespoons all-purpose flour
- 4 teaspoons sweet Hungarian paprika
- ½ teaspoon salt
- ¼ teaspoon black pepper
- 1 cup water or vegetable broth
- 1 can (8 ounces) tomato sauce
- ¼ cup sour cream
- Chopped fresh parsley

1. Cook pasta in large saucepan of salted boiling water according to package directions for al dente. Drain and return to saucepan; keep warm.
2. Heat oil in large skillet over medium heat. Add bell peppers, onion and garlic; cook and stir 8 to 10 minutes or until peppers are very soft. Sprinkle flour, paprika, salt and black pepper over vegetables. Gradually stir in water until smooth; stir in tomato sauce. Reduce heat to low; simmer about 5 minutes or until sauce thickens.
3. Remove skillet from heat. Place sour cream in small bowl; stir in several spoonfuls hot mixture. Stir sour cream mixture into sauce in skillet. Pour sauce over pasta; stir until well blended. Top with parsley.

Roasted Salmon and Asparagus with Quinoa

MAKES 4 SERVINGS

- 1 pound fresh asparagus spears
- 4 teaspoons olive oil, divided
- 12 to 16 ounces salmon fillets
- 1½ teaspoons salt, divided
- ¼ teaspoon black pepper, divided
- ½ cup uncooked quinoa
- 1 cup water
- 1 green onion, chopped
- 1 teaspoon lemon juice
- 1 teaspoon minced fresh dill
- 4 lemon wedges (optional)

1. Preheat oven to 400°F. Place asparagus in large nonstick roasting pan. Drizzle with 1 teaspoon oil. Roast 10 minutes. Turn asparagus and push to one side of pan. Arrange salmon, skin side down, on other side. Brush with 2 teaspoons oil, sprinkle with ½ teaspoon salt and ⅛ teaspoon pepper. Roast 10 to 13 minutes or until salmon is cooked through. Place asparagus on cutting board; cut into bite-size pieces.
2. Meanwhile, place quinoa in fine-mesh strainer; rinse well under cold water. Bring 1 cup water to a boil in small saucepan; stir in quinoa and ½ teaspoon salt. Reduce heat to low; cover and simmer 10 to 15 minutes or until quinoa is tender and water is absorbed. Transfer to large bowl.
3. Stir in asparagus, green onion, remaining 1 teaspoon oil, ½ teaspoon salt, ⅛ teaspoon pepper, lemon juice and dill. Transfer to four plates; top with salmon. Garnish with lemon wedges.

Multicooker Magic

Chicken Adobo

MAKES 4 SERVINGS

- ⅓ cup cider vinegar
- ⅓ cup soy sauce
- 5 cloves garlic, minced
- 3 bay leaves
- 1 teaspoon black pepper
- 2½ to 3 pounds bone-in skin-on chicken thighs

Pressure Cooker Directions

1 Combine vinegar, soy sauce, garlic, bay leaves and pepper in pot; mix well. Add chicken; turn to coat. Arrange chicken skin side down in liquid.

2 Secure lid and move pressure release valve to sealing or locked position. Cook at high pressure 13 minutes. Preheat broiler. Line baking sheet with foil.

3 When cooking is complete, use natural release for 10 minutes, then release remaining pressure. Remove chicken to prepared baking sheet, skin side up.

4 Broil chicken about 4 minutes or until skin is browned and crisp. Meanwhile, press Sauté; cook liquid in pot about 5 minutes or until slightly reduced. Pour sauce over chicken.

Stovetop Directions

Prepare ingredients as directed in step 1 in large saucepan. Bring to a boil over high heat. Reduce heat to low; cover and simmer 30 minutes. Turn chicken skin side up. Cook, uncovered, 20 minutes. Broil as directed in step 4. Cook liquid in saucepan over medium heat 10 minutes or until reduced and thickened.

Orecchiette with Sausage and Broccoli Rabe

MAKES 4 TO 6 SERVINGS

- 1 tablespoon olive oil
- 12 ounces bulk mild Italian sausage
- 1 bunch broccoli rabe (about 1 pound), tough stems removed, cut into 2-inch pieces
- 3 cloves garlic, minced
- ¼ teaspoon red pepper flakes
- ¼ cup dry white wine
- 1 package (16 ounces) uncooked orecchiette pasta
- 4 cups chicken broth
- ⅓ cup water
- 1 teaspoon salt
- ¾ cup grated Parmesan cheese, divided
- Juice of 1 lemon

Pressure Cooker Directions

1 Press Sauté; heat oil in pot. Add sausage; cook about 8 minutes or until browned, stirring to break up meat. Remove to plate with slotted spoon. Add broccoli rabe to pot; cook and stir 5 minutes or until crisp-tender. Transfer to bowl; cover to keep warm.

2 Return sausage to pot. Add garlic and red pepper flakes; cook and stir 1 minute. Add wine; cook 2 minutes, stirring to scrape up browned bits. Stir in pasta, broth, water and salt; mix well.

3 Secure lid and move pressure release valve to sealing or locked position. Cook at high pressure 5 minutes.

4 When cooking is complete, use quick release. Stir in broccoli rabe, ½ cup cheese and lemon juice; mix well. Serve immediately with remaining cheese.

Stovetop Directions

Cook pasta according to package directions. Drain, reserving 1 cup cooking water. Cook ingredients as directed in step 1 in large skillet over medium-high heat. Add garlic and red pepper flakes; cook and stir 1 minute. Add wine, stirring to scrape up browned bits. Return sausage and broccoli rabe to skillet. Add pasta, cheese, lemon juice and ½ cup pasta water; cook and stir until heated through and saucy, adding additional water if needed.

Smokehouse Barbecue Brisket

MAKES 6 SERVINGS

- 1 beef brisket (3 to 3½ pounds)
- 2 teaspoons salt
- 2 teaspoons garlic powder
- 2 teaspoons onion powder
- 2 teaspoons smoked paprika
- 1 teaspoon black pepper
- 1 can (6 ounces) tomato sauce
- ½ cup ketchup
- ¼ cup cider vinegar
- ¼ cup packed dark brown sugar
- 1½ tablespoons Worcestershire sauce
- 1½ teaspoons liquid smoke
- ½ teaspoon ground red pepper
- 2 tablespoons vegetable oil
- ½ cup beef broth
- Kaiser rolls or hamburger buns

Pressure Cooker Directions

1 Trim fat on brisket to ¼ inch. Combine salt, garlic powder, onion powder, smoked paprika and black pepper in small bowl; mix well. Rub mixture all over brisket; set aside. Combine tomato sauce, ketchup, vinegar, brown sugar, Worcestershire sauce, liquid smoke and red pepper in medium bowl; mix well.

2 Press Sauté; heat oil in pot. Add brisket; cook 4 to 5 minutes per side or until browned. Remove to plate. Add broth to pot; cook 1 minute, stirring to scrape up browned bits. Stir in tomato sauce mixture until blended. Return brisket to pot; turn to coat with sauce.

3 Secure lid and move pressure release valve to sealing or locked position. Cook at high pressure 70 minutes.

4 When cooking is complete, use natural release for 15 minutes, then release remaining pressure. Remove brisket to cutting board; let stand 15 minutes. Meanwhile, press Sauté; cook sauce in pot about 15 minutes or until reduced by half, skimming fat from top of sauce frequently.

5 Slice brisket against the grain. Return brisket to pot. Turn off heat; cover and let stand 15 to 20 minutes. Serve on rolls.

Oven Directions

Preheat oven to 250°F. Prepare ingredients as directed in steps 1 and 2 in Dutch oven over medium-high heat. Cover and bake 5 hours or until falling apart, basting every 30 minutes. Remove brisket to cutting board; let stand 15 minutes. Slice ½ inch thick; return slices to Dutch oven. Bake 30 minutes.

Meaty Sausage Spaghetti

MAKES 6 TO 8 SERVINGS

- 1 tablespoon olive oil
- 1 medium onion, chopped
- 2 cloves garlic, minced
- 1 package (20 ounces) bulk Italian sausage
- 1 cup chopped yellow, red and/or green bell peppers
- 1 can (about 14 ounces) crushed tomatoes
- 1 can (about 14 ounces) diced tomatoes
- 2½ teaspoons salt
- 2 teaspoons dried basil
- 1 teaspoon dried oregano
- ¼ teaspoon black pepper
- 1 package (16 ounces) uncooked spaghetti, broken in half
- 2½ to 3½ cups water, divided
- Grated Parmesan cheese

Pressure Cooker Directions

1 Press Sauté; heat oil in pot. Add onion and garlic; cook and stir 3 minutes or until onion is softened. Add sausage; cook until browned, stirring to break up meat. Drain fat. Add bell peppers; cook and stir 2 minutes. Add crushed tomatoes, diced tomatoes, salt, basil, oregano and black pepper; mix well. Add pasta; stir gently to allow some liquid to get between strands of spaghetti to prevent sticking. Add 2½ cups water.

2 Secure lid and move pressure release valve to sealing or locked position. Cook at high pressure 5 minutes.

3 When cooking is complete, use quick release. Press Sauté; add ½ cup water. Cook and stir 2 minutes or until pasta is al dente, adding remaining ½ cup water if necessary to reach desired sauce consistency. Serve with cheese.

Stovetop Directions

Cook ingredients as directed in step 1 in large saucepan or Dutch oven over medium-high heat. Bring to a boil. Reduce heat to medium; cover and cook 15 minutes, stirring occasionally to separate spaghetti. Uncover; stir in additional water if pasta seems dry. Test for doneness; continue to cook 3 minutes or until pasta is desired doneness, stirring frequently.

Chickpea Tikka Masala

MAKES 4 SERVINGS

- 1¼ cups dried chickpeas, soaked 8 hours or overnight
- 1 tablespoon olive oil
- 1 onion, chopped
- 3 cloves garlic, minced
- 1 tablespoon minced fresh ginger
- 1 tablespoon garam masala
- 1½ teaspoons salt
- 1 teaspoon ground coriander
- 1 teaspoon ground cumin
- ¼ teaspoon ground red pepper
- 1 can (28 ounces) crushed tomatoes
- 1 can (about 13 ounces) unsweetened coconut milk
- 1 package (about 12 ounces) paneer cheese or silken tofu, cut into 1-inch cubes
- Hot cooked basmati rice (optional)
- Chopped fresh cilantro

Pressure Cooker Directions

1 Drain and rinse chickpeas. Press Sauté; heat oil in pot. Add onion; cook and stir 5 minutes or until translucent. Add garlic, ginger, garam masala, salt, coriander, cumin and red pepper; cook and stir 1 minute. Stir in chickpeas, tomatoes and coconut milk; mix well.

2 Secure lid and move pressure release valve to sealing or locked position. Cook at high pressure 22 minutes.

3 When cooking is complete, use natural release for 10 minutes, then release remaining pressure.

4 Press Sauté; adjust heat to low. Add paneer to pot; stir gently. Cook 5 minutes or until paneer is heated through, stirring occasionally. Serve with rice, if desired; garnish with cilantro.

Stovetop Directions

Substitute 2 cans (15 ounces each) chickpeas, rinsed and drained, for the dried chickpeas. Cook ingredients as directed in step 1 in large saucepan over medium-high heat. Reduce heat to medium; simmer 30 minutes or until sauce is thickened and chickpeas have softened slightly. Add paneer; stir gently. Cook 7 to 10 minutes or until paneer is heated through.

Italian Beef Sandwiches

MAKES 4 SERVINGS

- 1 jar (16 ounces) sliced pepperoncini peppers
- 1 jar (16 ounces) giardiniera
- 2 to 2½ pounds boneless beef chuck roast
- ½ cup beef broth
- 1 tablespoon Italian seasoning
- 4 French or sub rolls, split

Pressure Cooker Directions

1 Drain pepperoncini, reserving ½ cup liquid. Set aside ½ cup pepperoncini for sandwiches. Drain giardiniera, reserving ½ cup vegetables for sandwiches.

2 Combine beef, remaining pepperoncini and reserved ½ cup pepperoncini liquid, remaining giardiniera vegetables, broth and Italian seasoning in pot.

3 Secure lid and move pressure release valve to sealing or locked position. Cook at high pressure 60 minutes.

4 When cooking is complete, use natural release for 15 minutes, then release remaining pressure. Remove beef to large bowl; let stand until cool enough to handle. Shred beef into bite-size pieces. Add ½ cup cooking liquid; stir to coat.

5 Fill rolls with beef, reserved pepperoncini and reserved giardiniera vegetables. Serve with warm cooking liquid for dipping.

Oven Directions

Preheat oven to 325°F. Prepare ingredients as directed in step 1. Cut beef into four pieces; season with salt and pepper. Heat 1 tablespoon olive oil in Dutch oven over medium-high heat. Add beef; cook 8 to 10 minutes per side or until well browned. Remove to plate. Drain fat. Add ¼ cup broth to Dutch oven; cook 1 minute, stirring to scrape up browned bits. Stir in another 1 cup broth, remaining pepperoncini with liquid, remaining giardiniera vegetables and Italian seasoning; bring to a boil. Return beef to Dutch oven. (Beef should be about half submerged in liquid; add water or additional broth if necessary.) Cover and bake 2½ to 3 hours or until beef is tender. Remove beef to cutting board; let stand until cool enough to handle. Shred beef into bite-size pieces. Add ¾ cup cooking liquid; stir to coat.

Vegetarian Chili

MAKES 8 TO 10 SERVINGS

- 2 tablespoons olive oil
- 1 onion, finely chopped
- 2 medium carrots, chopped
- 1 red bell pepper, chopped
- 3 tablespoons chili powder
- 2 tablespoons tomato paste
- 2 tablespoons packed brown sugar
- 2 tablespoons ground cumin
- 3 cloves garlic, minced
- 1 tablespoon dried oregano
- 2 teaspoons salt
- 1 can (28 ounces) diced tomatoes
- 1 can (15 ounces) tomato sauce
- 1 can (about 15 ounces) small white beans, rinsed and drained
- 2 cans (about 15 ounces each) kidney beans, rinsed and drained
- 1 can (about 15 ounces) pinto beans, rinsed and drained
- 1 can (4 ounces) diced mild green chiles
- 1 ounce unsweetened chocolate, chopped
- 1 tablespoon cider vinegar

Pressure Cooker Directions

1 Press Sauté; heat oil in pot. Add onion, carrots and bell pepper; cook and stir 5 minutes or until vegetables are softened. Add chili powder, tomato paste, brown sugar, cumin, garlic, oregano and salt; cook and stir 1 minute. Stir in tomatoes, tomato sauce, beans and chiles; mix well.

2 Secure lid and move pressure release valve to sealing or locked position. Cook at high pressure 10 minutes.

3 When cooking is complete, use natural release for 10 minutes, then release remaining pressure. Stir in chocolate and vinegar until blended.

Stovetop Directions

Cook ingredients as directed in step 1 in large saucepan or Dutch oven over medium-high heat. Bring to a boil. Reduce heat to medium; simmer 20 minutes, stirring occasionally. Stir in chocolate and vinegar just before serving.

Butter Chicken

MAKES 4 TO 6 SERVINGS

- 2 tablespoons butter
- 1 onion, chopped
- 4 cloves garlic, minced
- 1 teaspoon minced fresh ginger
- 1 teaspoon ground turmeric
- 1 teaspoon ground coriander
- 1 teaspoon garam masala
- 1 teaspoon ground cumin
- ½ teaspoon ground red pepper
- ½ teaspoon paprika
- 1 can (about 14 ounces) diced tomatoes
- ¾ teaspoon salt
- 2 pounds boneless skinless chicken breasts, cut into 2-inch pieces
- ½ cup whipping cream
- Chopped fresh cilantro
- Hot cooked rice

Pressure Cooker Directions

1 Press Sauté; melt butter in pot. Add onion; cook and stir about 4 minutes or until onion begins to turn golden. Add garlic and ginger; cook and stir 1 minute. Add turmeric, coriander, garam masala, cumin, red pepper and paprika; cook and stir 30 seconds. Add tomatoes and salt; cook and stir 2 minutes. Stir in chicken; mix well.

2 Secure lid and move pressure release valve to sealing or locked position. Cook at high pressure 8 minutes.

3 When cooking is complete, use natural release for 10 minutes, then release remaining pressure.

4 Press Sauté; adjust heat to low. Stir in cream; cook 5 minutes or until heated through. Sprinkle with cilantro; serve with rice.

Stovetop Directions

Cook ingredients as directed in step 1 in large saucepan over medium-high heat. Reduce heat to medium-low; cover and simmer 15 minutes or until chicken is cooked through (165°F). Stir in cream; cook and stir 5 minutes.

Pumpkin Risotto

MAKES 4 SERVINGS

- 2 tablespoons butter
- 1 tablespoon olive oil
- 1 onion, finely chopped
- 2 cloves garlic, minced
- 1½ cups uncooked arborio rice
- 1 teaspoon salt
- ¼ teaspoon ground nutmeg
- ⅛ teaspoon black pepper
- ½ cup dry white wine
- 4 cups vegetable broth
- 1 can (15 ounces) pumpkin purée
- 5 fresh sage leaves
- ½ cup shredded Parmesan cheese, plus additional for serving
- ¼ cup pepitas

Pressure Cooker Directions

1. Press Sauté; heat butter and oil in pot. Add onion and garlic; cook and stir 3 minutes or until softened. Add rice; cook and stir 4 minutes or until rice is translucent. Stir in salt, nutmeg and pepper. Add wine; cook and stir about 1 minute or until evaporated. Stir in broth, pumpkin and sage; mix well.
2. Secure lid and move pressure release valve to sealing or locked position. Cook at high pressure 6 minutes.
3. When cooking is complete, use quick release.
4. Press Sauté; adjust heat to low. Cook about 3 minutes or until risotto reaches desired consistency, stirring constantly. Stir in ½ cup cheese until blended. Serve immediately with additional cheese and pepitas.

Stovetop Directions

Combine broth, whole sage leaves and nutmeg in small saucepan; bring to a boil over high heat. Reduce heat to low to maintain a simmer. Cook ingredients as directed in step 1 in large saucepan over medium-high heat (do not add broth, pumpkin and sage). Add broth mixture ½ cup at a time, stirring frequently until broth is absorbed before adding next ½ cup (discard sage). Stir in pumpkin when about 1 cup broth remains. Add remaining broth; cook until rice is al dente, stirring constantly. (Total cook time will be about 25 minutes.) Remove from heat; stir in ½ cup cheese and 1 tablespoon chopped sage.

Chorizo Burritos

MAKES 4 TO 5 SERVINGS

- 15 ounces Mexican-style chorizo sausage, cut into bite-size pieces
- 1 can (about 15 ounces) red beans, rinsed and drained
- 1 can (about 14 ounces) diced tomatoes
- 1 can (11 ounces) corn, drained
- 2 green or red bell peppers, cut into 1-inch pieces
- 1 cup chicken broth
- ½ teaspoon ground cumin
- ½ teaspoon ground cinnamon
- 8 to 10 fajita-size flour tortillas, warmed (9 to 10 inches)
- 1 cup hot cooked rice
- Shredded Monterey Jack cheese and/or sour cream

Slow Cooker Directions

1 Combine chorizo, beans, tomatoes, corn, bell peppers, broth, cumin and cinnamon in slow cooker; mix well. Cover; cook on LOW 6 to 8 hours.

2 Spoon chorizo filling down centers of warm tortillas; top with rice and shredded cheese. Roll up and serve immediately.

Pressure Cooker Directions

Combine chorizo, beans, tomatoes, corn, bell peppers, cumin and cinnamon in pot; mix well. Secure lid and move pressure release valve to sealing or locked position. Cook at high pressure 10 minutes. When cooking is complete, use natural release for 10 minutes, then release remaining pressure. Press Sauté; cook about 5 minutes or until chorizo mixture thickens, stirring occasionally.

Coq au Vin

MAKES 4 TO 6 SERVINGS

- 4 slices thick-cut bacon, cut into ½-inch pieces
- 8 bone-in skinless chicken thighs (3½ to 4 pounds)
- 1 teaspoon salt
- ½ teaspoon black pepper
- 1 package (8 to 10 ounces) cremini mushrooms, quartered
- 3 carrots, cut into 1½-inch pieces
- 1 tablespoon tomato paste
- 2 cloves garlic, minced
- 10 sprigs fresh thyme
- 1½ cups dry red wine
- 8 ounces frozen pearl onions (about 1½ cups), divided
- 1 bay leaf
- 1 tablespoon butter, softened
- 1 tablespoon all-purpose flour
- Chopped fresh parsley (optional)

Pressure Cooker Directions

1 Press Sauté; cook bacon in pot until crisp. Remove to paper towel-lined plate.

2 Season both sides of chicken with 1 teaspoon salt and ½ teaspoon pepper. Add chicken to drippings in pot in two batches; cook 3 to 4 minutes per side or until browned. Remove to plate.

3 Add mushrooms and carrots to pot; cook about 6 minutes or until mushrooms have given off their liquid and begin to brown, stirring occasionally and scraping up browned bits from bottom of pot. Add tomato paste, garlic and thyme; cook and stir 2 minutes. Stir in wine; cook 10 minutes or until reduced by half. Return chicken to pot with half of onions, half of bacon and bay leaf.

4 Secure lid and move pressure release valve to sealing or locked position. Cook at high pressure 14 minutes. Meanwhile, mix butter and flour in small bowl.

5 When cooking is complete, use quick release. Remove chicken and vegetables to platter with slotted spoon. Remove and discard thyme sprigs and bay leaf.

6 Press Sauté; add butter mixture and remaining half of onions to pot. Cook and stir 2 to 3 minutes or until sauce thickens. Pour sauce over chicken and vegetables. Garnish with reserved bacon and parsley, if desired.

Slow Cooker Directions

Prepare ingredients as directed in steps 1 through 3 in large skillet over medium-high heat, removing chicken to slow cooker and pouring sauce over chicken. Cover and cook on LOW 8 to 10 hours or on HIGH 3 to 4 hours. Remove chicken and vegetables to platter with slotted spoon. Remove and discard thyme sprigs and bay leaf. Combine butter and flour in small bowl. Add butter mixture and remaining half of onions to slow cooker; cook on HIGH 15 minutes or until thickened, stirring frequently.

Mushroom Rice Pilaf

MAKES 6 TO 8 SERVINGS

- 2 cups uncooked long grain rice
- 1 tablespoon olive oil
- 1 medium onion, chopped
- 1¼ cups sliced cremini mushrooms
- 2 tablespoons butter
- 1⅔ cups vegetable broth
- ⅓ cup dry red wine
- ½ teaspoon salt
- ¼ teaspoon black pepper
- 1 medium zucchini, thinly sliced

Pressure Cooker Directions

1. Rinse rice well; drain in fine-mesh strainer.
2. Press Sauté; heat oil in pot. Add onion; cook and stir 3 minutes or until softened. Add mushrooms; cook and stir 4 minutes. Add rice and butter; cook 5 minutes or until rice begins to turn golden, stirring frequently. Stir in broth, wine, salt and pepper; mix well.
3. Secure lid and move pressure release valve to sealing or locked position. Cook at high pressure 4 minutes.
4. When cooking is complete, use natural release for 10 minutes, then release remaining pressure.
5. Press Sauté. Add zucchini; cook about 2 minutes or until zucchini is crisp-tender, stirring frequently.

Slow Cooker Directions

Heat oil in large skillet over medium heat. Add rice, onion, mushrooms and zucchini; cook and stir 4 to 5 minutes or until rice is slightly browned and onion is tender. Transfer to slow cooker. Add broth, wine, salt and pepper. Drizzle melted butter over top; stir once. Cover and cook on LOW 6 to 8 hours.

Air-Fried Favorites

Chicken Pesto Flatbreads

MAKES 2 SERVINGS

- 2 boneless skinless chicken breasts (3 to 4 ounces each)
- Salt and black pepper
- 2 (6- to 7-inch) round flatbreads or Greek-style pita bread rounds
- 2 tablespoons pesto
- 4 slices (1 ounce each) mozzarella cheese
- 1 plum tomato, sliced
- ¼ cup shredded Parmesan cheese

1. Preheat air fryer to 370°F. Spray basket with nonstick cooking spray.
2. Season chicken with salt and pepper. Cook 12 to 15 minutes or until no longer pink in center and cooked through (165°F). Cool slightly; slice chicken.
3. Place flatbreads on work surface. Spread 1 tablespoon pesto over half of each flatbread. Place half of chicken on opposite half of bread; top each with half of mozzarella cheese, tomato and Parmesan cheese. Fold in half.
4. Spray flatbread with cooking spray. Cook sandwiches 2 to 3 minutes per side or until flatbread is browned and cheese begins to melt.

Stovetop Directions

Spread 1 tablespoon pesto over half of each flatbread. Place 1 cup packaged grilled chicken on opposite half of bread; top with mozzarella cheese, tomato and Parmesan cheese. Fold in half. Spray grill pan or nonstick skillet with nonstick cooking spray; heat over medium-high heat. Cook sandwiches 3 minutes per side or until bread is toasted and cheese begins to melt.

Chorizo Quesadillas

MAKES 6 SERVINGS

- 1 package (9 ounces) uncooked regular or vegetarian Mexican chorizo sausage, casings removed
- 1 cup coarsely chopped cauliflower
- 1 small onion, finely chopped
- 12 (6-inch) flour tortillas
- 1½ cups (6 ounces) grated chihuahua cheese
- Salsa, guacamole and sour cream (optional)

1 Heat medium skillet over medium-high heat. Add chorizo, cauliflower and onion; cook and stir 10 to 12 minutes or until cauliflower is tender.

2 Place six tortillas on work surface. Spread ¼ cup chorizo mixture over each tortilla; top with ¼ cup cheese and remaining tortillas.

3 Preheat air fryer to 350°F. Spray basket with nonstick cooking spray. Place one quesadilla in basket; spray with nonstick cooking spray. Place metal trivet, measuring cup or butter knife on top of quesadilla (to prevent top tortilla from blowing off).

4 Cook 4 minutes; turn and cook 2 to 3 minutes or until lightly browned. Repeat with remaining quesadillas. Cut into wedges; serve with salsa, guacamole and sour cream, if desired.

Stovetop Directions

Heat medium skillet over medium-high heat. Add chorizo, cauliflower and onion; cook and stir 10 to 12 minutes or until cauliflower is tender. Remove to bowl. Wipe out skillet. Spread ¼ cup chorizo mixture on each of six tortillas. Top with ¼ cup cheese and remaining six tortillas. Heat 1 teaspoon oil in same skillet over medium-high heat. Add one quesadilla; cook 2 to 3 minutes per side or until well browned and cheese is melted. Repeat with remaining oil and quesadillas.

Peri-Peri Chicken

MAKES 4 SERVINGS

- 1 small red onion, coarsely chopped
- 1 roasted red pepper (about 3 ounces)
- ¼ cup olive oil
- ¼ cup lemon juice
- 2 tablespoons white vinegar
- 4 cloves garlic, minced
- 1 tablespoon smoked paprika
- 1½ teaspoons salt
- 1½ teaspoons red pepper flakes
- 1 teaspoon dried oregano
- ½ teaspoon black pepper
- 1 cut-up whole chicken (3 to 4 pounds)

1 Combine onion, roasted pepper, oil, lemon juice, vinegar, garlic, paprika, salt, red pepper flakes, oregano and black pepper in blender or food processor; blend until smooth. Remove half of marinade to small bowl; cover and refrigerate until ready to use.

2 Use sharp knife to make several slashes in each piece of chicken (about ¼ inch deep). Place chicken in large resealable food storage bag. Pour remaining marinade over chicken; seal bag and turn to coat, massaging marinade into chicken. Marinate chicken in refrigerator at least 4 hours or overnight, turning occasionally.

3 Remove chicken from refrigerator about 30 minutes before cooking. Preheat air fryer to 370°F. Spray basket with nonstick cooking spray.

4 Cook chicken 20 to 25 minutes or until cooked through (165°F), brushing with some of reserved marinade every 15 minutes. Serve with remaining marinade, if desired.

Oven Directions

Prepare marinade and chicken as directed through step 2. Remove chicken from refrigerator about 30 minutes before cooking. Preheat oven to 400°F. Line baking sheet with foil. Arrange chicken on baking sheet. Bake about 45 minutes or until chicken is cooked through (165°F), brushing with some of reserved marinade every 15 minutes. (For a smokier flavor, grill chicken over medium heat 40 to 45 minutes instead of baking.)

Blackened Chicken Torta

MAKES 4 SERVINGS

- 2 tablespoons vegetable oil
- 1½ tablespoons Creole seasoning
- 4 boneless skinless chicken breasts (6 to 8 ounces each)
- ½ cup sour cream
- 2 teaspoons lime juice, divided
- ½ teaspoon ground cumin
- ¼ teaspoon salt, divided
- Dash black pepper
- ⅓ cup mayonnaise
- ½ teaspoon chipotle chili powder
- 1 ripe avocado
- 4 slices (1 ounce each) Cheddar cheese
- 4 slices (1 ounce each) pepper Jack cheese
- 4 ciabatta rolls, split
- 1 cup finely shredded green cabbage or coleslaw mix

1. Combine oil and Creole seasoning in shallow dish; mix well. Add chicken; turn to coat completely with spice mixture. Let stand while preparing sauces.
2. Combine sour cream, 1½ teaspoons lime juice, cumin, ⅛ teaspoon salt and dash of pepper in medium bowl; mix well. Combine mayonnaise, remaining ½ teaspoon lime juice, ⅛ teaspoon salt and chipotle chili powder in small bowl. Mash avocado in another small bowl; season with additional salt and pepper.
3. Preheat air fryer to 370°F. Spray basket with nonstick cooking spray.
4. Cook chicken 12 to 15 minutes or until no longer pink in center (165°F). Remove to plate; top each chicken breast with 1 slice of Cheddar and 1 slice of pepper Jack. Tent loosely with foil to melt cheese.
5. For each sandwich, spread 2 tablespoons sour cream mixture on bottom half of roll; top with mashed avocado. Layer with ¼ cup cabbage and chicken. Spread heaping tablespoon mayonnaise mixture on top half of roll; close sandwich.

Stovetop Directions

Prepare chicken and sauce as directed through step 2. Heat cast iron skillet over medium-high heat until very hot. Add chicken; cook about 6 minutes per side or until well browned and cooked through (165°F). Remove to cutting board; top each chicken breast with 1 slice of Cheddar and 1 slice of pepper Jack cheese. Tent loosely with foil to melt cheese. Proceed with step 5.

Spicy Crispy Shrimp

MAKES 4 SERVINGS

- ½ cup mayonnaise
- 4 teaspoons Thai chili sauce
- 1 teaspoon honey
- ½ teaspoon rice vinegar
- ¾ cup buttermilk
- 1 egg
- ¾ cup all-purpose flour
- ½ cup panko bread crumbs
- 1 teaspoon salt
- ½ teaspoon ground sage
- ½ teaspoon black pepper
- ¼ teaspoon onion powder
- ¼ teaspoon garlic powder
- ¼ teaspoon dried basil
- 16 large raw shrimp, peeled, deveined and patted dry
- Sliced green onions (optional)

1. For sauce, combine mayonnaise, chili sauce, honey and vinegar in small bowl; mix well. Cover and refrigerate until ready to serve.
2. Whisk buttermilk and egg in medium bowl until well blended. Combine flour, panko, salt, sage, pepper, onion powder, garlic powder and basil in separate medium bowl; mix well. Dip each shrimp in buttermilk mixture, then in flour mixture, turning to coat completely. Place breaded shrimp on large plate; refrigerate 15 minutes.
3. Preheat air fryer to 390°F. Spray basket with nonstick cooking spray. Cook shrimp in batches 6 to 8 minutes or until golden brown, turning halfway through cooking.
4. Transfer shrimp to large bowl; add sauce and toss gently to coat. Garnish with green onions.

Stovetop Directions

Prepare sauce and shrimp as directed through step 2. Heat 2 inches of oil in large saucepan over medium-high heat to 350°F; adjust heat to maintain temperature during cooking. Cook shrimp in batches 2 to 3 minutes or until golden brown, turning once. Drain on paper towel-lined plate. Transfer shrimp to large bowl; add sauce and toss gently to coat.

Teriyaki Salmon

MAKES 2 SERVINGS

- ¼ cup toasted sesame oil
- Juice of 1 lemon
- ¼ cup soy sauce
- 2 tablespoons packed brown sugar
- 1 clove garlic, minced
- 2 salmon fillets (about 4 ounces each)
- Hot cooked rice
- Toasted sesame seeds and sliced green onions (optional)

1. Whisk oil, lemon juice, soy sauce, brown sugar and garlic in medium bowl until well blended. Place salmon in large resealable food storage bag. Pour marinade over salmon; seal bag and turn to coat. Marinate in refrigerator at least 2 hours.
2. Preheat air fryer to 390°F. Spray basket with nonstick cooking spray.
3. Cook salmon 8 to 10 minutes or until crisp and begins to flake when tested with fork. Serve with rice; garnish with sesame seeds and green onions.

Grill Directions

Marinate salmon as directed in step 1. Preheat grill or broiler. Grill or broil salmon 6 to 8 minutes or until crisp and salmon begins to flake when tested with fork, turning once.

Blue Cheese Stuffed Chicken Breasts

MAKES 4 SERVINGS

- ½ cup crumbled blue cheese
- 2 tablespoons butter, softened, divided
- ¾ teaspoon dried thyme
- Salt and black pepper
- 4 bone-in skin-on chicken breasts
- 1 tablespoon lemon juice

1. Combine blue cheese, 1 tablespoon butter and thyme in small bowl; stir to blend. Season with salt and pepper.
2. Loosen chicken skin by pushing fingers between skin and meat, taking care not to tear skin. Spread cheese mixture under skin; massage skin to spread mixture evenly over chicken breast.
3. Melt remaining 1 tablespoon butter in small bowl; stir in lemon juice until blended. Brush mixture over chicken. Sprinkle with salt and pepper.
4. Preheat air fryer to 370°F. Cook chicken 15 to 20 minutes or until cooked through (165°F).

Oven Directions

Prepare chicken as directed through step 3. Preheat oven to 400°F. Arrange chicken on baking sheet. Bake 50 minutes or until cooked through (165°F).

Crispy Cornmeal Cauliflower Steaks

MAKES 4 SERVINGS

½ cup cornmeal
¼ cup all-purpose flour
1 teaspoon salt
1 teaspoon dried sage
½ teaspoon garlic powder
¼ teaspoon black pepper
½ cup milk
2 heads cauliflower
2 tablespoons butter, melted
Barbecue sauce (optional)

1 Combine cornmeal, flour, salt, sage, garlic powder and pepper in shallow dish; mix well. Pour milk into another shallow dish.

2 Turn cauliflower stem side up on cutting board. Trim away leaves, leaving stem intact. Slice through stem into three slices. Trim off excess florets from end slices, creating flat "steaks." Repeat with remaining cauliflower. Reserve extra cauliflower for another use.

3 Dip cauliflower into milk to coat both sides. Place in cornmeal mixture; pat onto all sides of cauliflower. Drizzle butter evenly over cauliflower.

4 Preheat air fryer to 390°F. Line basket with parchment paper.

5 Cook cauliflower in batches 12 to 15 minutes or until tender, turning halfway through cooking. Serve with barbecue sauce for dipping, if desired.

Oven Directions

Prepare cauliflower as directed through step 3. Preheat oven to 400°F. Line baking sheet with parchment paper. Place cauliflower on prepared baking sheet; drizzle evenly with butter. Bake 40 minutes or until cauliflower is tender.

Lemon Chicken

MAKES 4 SERVINGS

- 1 egg
- 2 teaspoons soy sauce
- 1½ cups panko bread crumbs
- ⅛ teaspoon salt
- ⅛ teaspoon black pepper
- 1 pound chicken tenders or 1 pound boneless skinless chicken breasts, cut into long 1-inch-thick strips
- 1 cup chicken broth
- 1 tablespoon cornstarch
- 1 teaspoon vegetable oil
- 1 clove garlic, minced
- Grated peel of 1 lemon
- 1 teaspoon sugar
- 1½ to 2½ teaspoons lemon juice

1 Whisk egg and soy sauce in shallow dish. Combine panko, salt and pepper in another shallow dish. Dip chicken strips in egg mixture, then roll in panko mixture to coat.

2 Preheat air fryer to 400°F. Spray basket with nonstick cooking spray. Working in batches, place chicken in single layer not touching in basket; spray with nonstick cooking spray.

3 Cook chicken 10 to 12 minutes or until golden brown and cooked through (165°F), turning halfway through cooking.

4 Meanwhile, stir broth into cornstarch in small bowl until smooth. Heat oil in small saucepan over low heat. Add garlic; cook and stir 1 minute or until softened. Stir in lemon peel. Add cornstarch mixture and sugar; cook and stir over medium heat 2 minutes or until thickened. Stir in 1½ teaspoons lemon juice. Drizzle sauce over chicken.

Oven Directions

Prepare chicken as directed in step 1. Preheat oven to 400°F. Line baking sheet with parchment paper. Arrange chicken on baking sheet in single layer; spray chicken with nonstick cooking spray. Bake 10 minutes; turn and bake 10 to 13 minutes or until chicken is golden brown and cooked through (165°F). Meanwhile, prepare sauce as directed in step 4.

Coconut Shrimp

MAKES 4 SERVINGS

Dipping Sauce

- ½ cup orange marmalade
- ⅓ cup Thai chili sauce
- 1 teaspoon prepared horseradish
- ½ teaspoon salt

Shrimp

- 1 cup flat beer
- 1 cup all-purpose flour
- 2 cups sweetened flaked coconut, divided
- 2 tablespoons sugar
- 16 to 20 large raw shrimp, peeled and deveined (with tails on), patted dry

1. For sauce, combine marmalade, chili sauce, horseradish and salt in small bowl; mix well.
2. For shrimp, whisk beer, flour, ½ cup coconut and sugar in large bowl until well blended. Place remaining 1½ cups coconut in medium bowl. Dip shrimp in batter, then in coconut, turning to coat completely.
3. Preheat air fryer to 390°F. Spray basket with nonstick cooking spray.
4. Cook shrimp in batches 6 to 8 minutes or until golden brown, turning halfway through cooking. Serve with dipping sauce.

Stovetop Directions

Prepare sauce and shrimp as directed through step 2. Heat 2 inches of oil in large saucepan over medium heat to 350°F; adjust heat to maintain temperature during cooking. Fry shrimp in batches 2 to 3 minutes or until golden brown, turning halfway through cooking time. Drain on paper towel-lined plate. Serve immediately with dipping sauce.

Milanese Pork Chops

MAKES 4 SERVINGS

2 tablespoons all-purpose flour
½ teaspoon salt
½ teaspoon black pepper
1 egg
1 teaspoon water
¼ cup seasoned dry bread crumbs
¼ cup grated Parmesan cheese
4 boneless pork loin chops, cut ¾ inch thick
Lemon wedges

1 Combine flour, salt and pepper in shallow bowl. Beat egg and water in second shallow bowl. Combine bread crumbs and Parmesan cheese in third shallow bowl.

2 Coat pork with flour mixture. Dip in egg mixture, letting excess drip back into bowl. Roll in bread crumb mixture to coat, pressing coating onto pork. Place on waxed paper; refrigerate 15 minutes.

3 Preheat air fryer to 400°F. Place pork chops in single layer in basket; spray lightly with nonstick cooking spray. Cook 7 minutes; turn and cook 5 minutes or until cooked through (145°F). Let stand 5 minutes before serving. Serve with lemon wedges.

Oven Directions

Prepare pork as directed through step 2. Preheat oven to 400°F. Heat oil and butter in large ovenproof skillet over medium-high heat until bubbly. Add pork; cook 4 minutes or until golden brown. Turn pork and transfer skillet to oven. Bake 6 to 8 minutes or until cooked through (145°F).

Parmesan-Crusted Tilapia

MAKES 6 SERVINGS

- ⅔ cup plus 2 tablespoons grated Parmesan cheese, divided
- ⅔ cup panko bread crumbs
- ⅓ cup prepared Alfredo sauce (refrigerated or jarred)
- 1½ teaspoons dried parsley flakes
- 6 tilapia fillets (4 ounces each)
- Shaved Parmesan cheese and minced fresh parsley (optional)

1. Combine ⅔ cup grated Parmesan cheese and panko in medium bowl; mix well. Combine Alfredo sauce, remaining 2 tablespoons grated cheese and parsley flakes in small bowl; mix well.
2. Spread Alfredo sauce mixture over top of fish, coating in thick even layer. Top with panko mixture, pressing gently to adhere.
3. Preheat air fryer to 390°F. Spray basket with nonstick cooking spray.
4. Cook fish in batches 8 to 10 minutes or until crust is golden brown and fish begins to flake when tested with fork. Garnish with shaved Parmesan cheese and fresh parsley.

Oven Directions

Prepare fish as directed through step 2. Preheat oven to 425°F. Line baking sheet with foil; spray foil with nonstick cooking spray. Place fish on prepared baking sheet. Bake on top rack of oven 15 minutes or until crust is golden brown and fish begins to flake when tested with fork.

Leveraging Leftovers

Cheesy Chicken Bake

MAKES 4 SERVINGS

- 1 package (16 ounces) refrigerated or thawed frozen pizza dough, at room temperature
- ½ cup plus 4 teaspoons Caesar salad dressing, divided
- 2 cups chopped cooked chicken
- 1 cup crumbled cooked bacon
- 1¼ cups (5 ounces) shredded Italian blend cheese or mozzarella cheese, divided

1 Preheat oven to 425°F. Line baking sheet with parchment paper.

2 Divide dough into four pieces. Roll out each piece into 7½×5-inch rectangle on lightly floured surface. Brush each piece with 2 tablespoons dressing, leaving ¼-inch border. Top with ½ cup chicken, ¼ cup bacon and ¼ cup cheese. Starting with long side, roll up jelly-roll style; pinch seams and ends to seal.

3 Place rolls seam side down on prepared baking sheet. Brush each roll with 1 teaspoon of remaining dressing; sprinkle with 1 tablespoon cheese.

4 Bake about 20 minutes or until golden brown. Serve warm.

Artichoke Turkey Noodle Bake

MAKES 6 SERVINGS

- 8 ounces uncooked wide egg noodles
- 2 tablespoons butter
- ½ cup finely chopped onion
- 1½ tablespoons all-purpose flour
- 1½ cans (12 ounces each) evaporated milk
- ¼ cup cream sherry*
- 1 can (about 14 ounces) stewed tomatoes, drained
- ½ teaspoon salt
- ¼ teaspoon black pepper
- Dash ground red pepper
- 2½ cups shredded cooked turkey or chicken
- 1 can (14 ounces) artichoke hearts, drained and thinly sliced
- 2 cups (8 ounces) shredded Cheddar cheese, divided
- ½ cup cooked crumbled turkey bacon or bacon (optional)

**You can substitute ¼ cup dry sherry mixed with 1 teaspoon packed brown sugar for the cream sherry, or use ¼ cup white wine.*

1. Preheat oven to 375°F. Spray 13×9-inch baking dish with nonstick cooking spray.
2. Cook noodles in large saucepan of salted boiling water according to package directions for al dente; drain and return to saucepan.
3. Meanwhile, melt butter in medium saucepan over medium high heat. Add onion; cook and stir 3 minutes or until tender. Add flour; cook and stir 1 minute. Gradually add evaporated milk and sherry; cook and stir 5 minutes or until thickened. Stir in tomatoes, salt, black pepper and red pepper; mix well.
4. Add sauce to noodles; stir in turkey, artichokes, 1 cup cheese and bacon, if desired. Spread in prepared baking dish; sprinkle with remaining 1 cup cheese.
5. Bake 40 minutes or until cheese is melted and casserole is heated through.

Chicken Fried Rice

MAKES 4 SERVINGS

- 2 tablespoons vegetable oil, divided
- 12 ounces boneless skinless chicken breasts, cut into ½-inch cubes
- Salt and black pepper
- 2 tablespoons butter
- 2 cloves garlic, minced
- ½ sweet onion, diced
- 1 medium carrot, diced
- 2 green onions, thinly sliced, plus additional for garnish
- 3 eggs
- 4 cups leftover cooked rice
- 3 tablespoons soy sauce
- 2 tablespoons sesame seeds

1. Heat 1 tablespoon oil in large skillet over medium-high heat. Add chicken; season with salt and pepper. Cook and stir 5 to 6 minutes or until cooked through. Add butter and garlic; cook and stir 1 minute or until butter is melted. Remove to medium bowl.
2. Add sweet onion, carrot and two green onions to skillet; cook and stir over high heat 3 minutes or until vegetables are softened. Add to bowl with chicken.
3. Heat remaining 1 tablespoon oil in same skillet. Crack eggs into skillet; cook and stir 45 seconds or until eggs are scrambled but still moist. Return chicken and vegetable mixture to skillet with rice, soy sauce and sesame seeds; cook and stir 2 minutes or until well blended and heated through. Season with additional salt and pepper; garnish with additional green onion.

Tip

If you have a taste for fried rice but don't have leftover rice, cook 1½ cups rice according to package directions without oil or butter. Spread hot rice on large rimmed baking sheet; cool to room temperature. Refrigerate several hours or overnight. Measure 4 cups for recipe.

Potato and Pork Frittata

MAKES 4 SERVINGS

- 12 ounces (about 3 cups) frozen hash brown potatoes
- 1 teaspoon Cajun seasoning
- 6 eggs
- ¼ cup milk
- 1 teaspoon dry mustard
- ½ teaspoon salt
- ¼ teaspoon black pepper
- 10 ounces (about 3 cups) frozen stir-fry vegetable blend
- ⅓ cup water
- ¾ cup chopped cooked pork
- ½ cup (2 ounces) shredded Cheddar cheese

1. Preheat oven to 400°F. Spray baking sheet with nonstick cooking spray. Spread potatoes on prepared baking sheet; sprinkle with Cajun seasoning. Bake 15 minutes or until hot. Remove from oven. *Reduce oven temperature to 350°F.*
2. Beat eggs, milk, mustard, salt and pepper in medium bowl until well blended. Combine vegetables and water in medium ovenproof nonstick skillet. Cook and stir over medium heat 5 minutes or until vegetables are crisp-tender; drain. Add potatoes and pork to vegetables in skillet; stir gently. Add egg mixture; sprinkle with cheese. Cook over medium-low heat 5 minutes.
3. Bake 5 minutes or until egg mixture is set and cheese is melted. Cut into wedges to serve.

Asian Basil Beef and Rice

MAKES 4 SERVINGS

- 1 tablespoon vegetable oil
- 2 cups sliced fresh mushrooms
- 1 pound cooked pot roast or other beef, cut into 1-inch pieces
- 1 pouch (about 9 ounces) teriyaki-flavored ready-to-serve rice
- 2 tablespoons water
- 1 tablespoon hoisin sauce or chili garlic sauce
- 1 teaspoon soy sauce
- 1 tablespoon sliced green onion
- 1 tablespoon minced fresh basil

1. Heat oil in large skillet over medium-high heat. Add mushrooms; stir-fry 5 minutes or until lightly browned. Add beef; stir-fry 2 minutes.
2. Crumble rice in bag. Add rice, water, hoisin sauce and soy sauce to beef mixture. Cover and cook over medium heat 3 to 5 minutes or until mixture is heated through. Stir in green onion and basil; serve immediately.

Tip

This is a great recipe to use up leftover pot roast or other type of beef. If you don't have leftover beef, cut 1 pound of boneless beef top sirloin steak crosswise into thin strips. Stir-fry with mushrooms in step 1.

Okonomiyaki (Savory Pancake)

MAKES 4 SERVINGS

- 2 eggs
- 1 cup all-purpose flour
- ½ teaspoon salt
- 1 cup finely chopped cabbage
- 2 green onions, chopped
- ¾ to 1 cup water
- 4 teaspoons vegetable oil
- Assorted fillings: chopped cooked chicken or beef, cubed tofu, sliced red bell pepper, asparagus, corn and/or mushrooms

Sauce

- ¼ cup ketchup
- 1½ tablespoons Worcestershire sauce
- 2 tablespoons sake
- 1 teaspoon tamari or soy sauce
- ¼ teaspoon Dijon mustard
- Mayonnaise (optional)

1. Whisk eggs, flour and salt in medium bowl until combined. (Some lumps are fine.) Stir in cabbage, ¾ cup water and green onions. Add enough additional water until batter is the consistency of thick pancake batter. Prepare fillings (about ⅓ cup of mixed fillings per pancake).
2. Heat large nonstick skillet over medium-high heat. Brush skillet with 1 teaspoon oil; pour in one fourth of batter and spread into circle. Cook 2 minutes; arrange fillings on top and press gently into batter with spatula. Cook 2 to 3 minutes or until edges of pancake look dull and underside is lightly browned. Turn pancake and continue cooking 2 to 4 minutes or until cooked through. Keep warm; repeat with remaining oil, batter and fillings.
3. Meanwhile for sauce, combine ketchup, Worcestershire sauce, sake, tamari and mustard in small saucepan. Simmer over medium-low heat 1 minute, stirring constantly. Let cool to room temperature.
4. Drizzle okonomiyaki with sauce and serve with mayonnaise, if desired.

Tip

Okonomiyaki is a popular Japanese snack food, enjoyed like pizza in bars and quick serve restaurants. Use any leftover vegetables or proteins you have on hand.

Leftover Turkey Caesar Salad with Homemade Croutons

MAKES 4 SERVINGS

- 4 slices (1 ounce each) whole grain bread, cut into ½-inch cubes
- 1 tablespoon olive oil
- ¼ teaspoon salt
- ¼ teaspoon dried basil
- ¼ teaspoon dried rosemary
- ¼ teaspoon dried thyme
- 6 cups chopped romaine lettuce
- 2 cups chopped cooked turkey or chicken
- ¼ cup shredded Parmesan cheese
- ¼ cup Caesar salad dressing

1. Preheat oven to 375°F. Combine bread cubes, oil, salt, basil, rosemary and thyme on large baking sheet; gently toss to coat. Arrange in single layer. Bake 12 minutes, stirring once. Cool completely.
2. Arrange lettuce on serving plates. Top evenly with turkey, croutons and cheese; drizzle with dressing.

Broccoli, Turkey and Noodle Skillet

MAKES 4 SERVINGS

- 1 tablespoon butter
- 1 green bell pepper, chopped
- 1 cup frozen chopped broccoli
- ¼ teaspoon black pepper
- 1½ cups chicken broth
- ½ cup milk or half-and-half
- 2 cups diced cooked turkey or chicken
- 1 package (about 4 ounces) chicken and broccoli pasta mix
- ¼ cup sour cream

1. Melt butter in large skillet over medium-high heat. Add bell pepper, broccoli and black pepper; cook and stir 5 minutes or until bell pepper is crisp-tender. Add broth and milk; bring to a boil. Stir in turkey and pasta mix.
2. Reduce heat to low. Cook 8 to 10 minutes or until noodles are tender, stirring frequently. Remove from heat. Stir in sour cream. Let stand 5 minutes or until sauce thickens.

Steak Hash

MAKES 4 SERVINGS

- 2 tablespoons vegetable oil
- 1 green bell pepper, chopped
- ½ medium onion, chopped
- 3 medium leftover baked potatoes, cut into bite-size pieces
- ½ pound leftover cooked steak or roast beef, cut into 1-inch pieces
- Salt and black pepper
- ¼ cup (1 ounce) shredded Monterey Jack cheese
- 1 tablespoon butter
- 4 eggs

1 Heat oil in large skillet over medium heat. Add bell pepper and onion; cook and stir 5 minutes or until crisp-tender. Stir in potatoes; reduce heat to low. Cover; cook about 10 minutes or until potatoes are heated through, stirring occasionally.

2 Stir in steak; season with salt and black pepper. Sprinkle with cheese. Cover; cook 5 minutes or until steak is heated through and cheese is melted.

3 Meanwhile, melt butter in medium nonstick skillet over medium heat. Add eggs; cook about 5 minutes or until whites are opaque and yolks are desired doneness. Top each serving of hash with one egg.

Quick Chicken Flautas

MAKES 4 SERVINGS

- 2 cups shredded cooked chicken*
- ⅔ cup chunky salsa
- 8 (6-inch) flour tortillas
- 2 to 3 tablespoons vegetable oil
- Sour cream and guacamole (optional)

**Use a supermarket rotisserie chicken for convenience; one chicken will yield about 4 cups shredded meat.*

1 Combine chicken and salsa in medium bowl; mix well. Place one tortilla on work surface; spread heaping ¼ cup chicken mixture on bottom half of tortilla. Roll up tightly into cylinder; secure with toothpick. Repeat with remaining tortillas and filling.

2 Heat 2 tablespoons oil in large skillet over medium-high heat. Add half of tortilla rolls, seam side down; cook 3 to 4 minutes or until lightly browned on bottom. Turn and cook 2 to 3 minutes or until browned. Remove to plate. Add remaining four tortilla rolls to skillet, adding additional 1 tablespoon oil if necessary.

3 Remove toothpicks. Serve immediately with sour cream and guacamole, if desired.

A Little Something Extra

Green Beans Gremolata

MAKES 8 SERVINGS

- 2 pounds fresh green beans, trimmed
- 3 tablespoons olive oil
- ½ cup grated Parmesan cheese
- ⅓ cup chopped fresh parsley
- 2 tablespoons grated lemon peel
- 3 cloves garlic, minced
- Salt and black pepper

1 Bring large pot of salted water to a boil. Add green beans; cook 3 minutes or until crisp-tender. Drain and place in large bowl. Add oil; toss to coat.

2 Combine Parmesan, parsley, lemon peel and garlic in medium bowl. Add to green beans; toss to coat. Season to taste with salt and pepper.

Crazy Good Breadsticks >

MAKES 16 BREADSTICKS

- ¼ cup (½ stick) butter, melted
- ¾ teaspoon garlic salt
- 1 container (about 14 ounces) refrigerated pizza dough
- ¼ cup grated Parmesan cheese
- Pizza sauce or marinara sauce (optional)

1 Preheat oven to 425°F. Line baking sheet with parchment paper. Combine butter and garlic salt in small bowl; mix well.

2 Unroll dough on prepared baking sheet. Cut crosswise into 16 strips; spread strips out slightly on baking sheet not touching. Brush with butter mixture.

3 Bake about 8 minutes or until golden brown. Immediately sprinkle with cheese. Serve warm with pizza sauce, if desired.

Cafeteria Noodles

MAKES 6 TO 8 SERVINGS

- 4 cups water
- 2 chicken bouillon cubes
- 1 package (16 ounces) wide egg noodles
- 1 can (10½ ounces) cream of chicken soup
- ½ cup (1 stick) butter, cut into pieces
- Salt and black pepper
- Chopped fresh parsley (optional)

1 Combine 4 cups water and bouillon cubes in large saucepan. Bring to a boil over high heat. Add noodles; return to a boil. Stir in soup; cook 2 minutes. Stir in butter. Remove from heat; cover and let stand 20 minutes.

2 Stir noodles; season to taste with salt and pepper. Sprinkle with parsley, if desired.

Crunchy Orange-Ginger Slaw

MAKES 6 TO 8 SERVINGS

- 1 package (3 ounces) ramen noodles, coarsely crumbled*
- 1 tablespoon sesame seeds
- 6 cups finely shredded green cabbage
- 2 cups shredded carrots
- ½ cup diced red onion
- ½ cup raisins
- ¾ cup orange marmalade, microwaved for 30 seconds
- ¼ cup cider vinegar
- ¼ cup canola oil
- 3 tablespoons grated fresh ginger
- 1 tablespoon soy sauce
- 1 teaspoon grated orange peel (optional)
- 1 teaspoon hot pepper sauce *or* ¼ teaspoon red pepper flakes
- ¼ teaspoon salt

**Use any flavor; discard seasoning packet.*

1 Heat medium skillet over medium-high heat. Add noodles and sesame seeds; cook 2 minutes or until lightly browned, stirring frequently. Transfer to plate.

2 Combine cabbage, carrots, onion and raisins in large bowl. Whisk marmalade, vinegar, oil, ginger, soy sauce, orange peel, if desired, hot pepper sauce and salt in medium bowl until well blended. Add to cabbage mixture; mix well. Cover and refrigerate at least 20 minutes.

3 Sprinkle with toasted noodles before serving.

Crunchy Kale Salad

MAKES 6 SERVINGS

- ¼ cup cider vinegar
- ¼ cup olive oil
- ¼ cup maple syrup
- 1 tablespoon lemon juice
- ½ tablespoon Dijon mustard
- ½ teaspoon salt
- ¼ teaspoon black pepper
- 10 cups chopped stemmed kale (about 1 large bunch)
- 2 cups shredded green cabbage
- ½ cup sliced almonds, toasted*

***To toast almonds, cook and stir in small skillet over medium-low heat 2 to 3 minutes or until fragrant.**

1 Whisk vinegar, oil, maple syrup, lemon juice, mustard, salt and pepper in small bowl or measuring cup until well blended.

2 Combine kale and cabbage in large bowl. Pour dressing over vegetables; massage kale with hands 3 to 4 minutes to soften.

3 Stir in almonds just before serving.

Cheese Biscuits

MAKES 24 BISCUITS

- 4 cups all-purpose flour
- 4½ teaspoons baking powder
- 1 tablespoon sugar
- 1 teaspoon salt
- ½ teaspoon baking soda
- 1 cup (2 sticks) cold butter, cut into pieces
- 2 cups (8 ounces) shredded Cheddar cheese
- ¾ cup (3 ounces) shredded Gruyère or Swiss cheese
- ⅓ cup grated Parmesan cheese
- 2 cups buttermilk
- 2 tablespoons butter, melted

1 Whisk flour, baking powder, sugar, salt and baking soda in large bowl. Cut in cold butter with pastry blender or fingertips until coarse crumbs form. Stir in Cheddar, Gruyère and Parmesan cheeses; toss to blend. Make a well in center of flour mixture; pour in buttermilk. Stir just until blended; do not overmix. Cover and refrigerate 20 minutes.

2 Preheat oven to 375°F. Line two large baking sheets with parchment paper. Scoop dough into 12 mounds onto each prepared baking sheet.

3 Bake 13 to 15 minutes or until golden brown. Brush melted butter over tops of biscuits. Serve warm.

Coleslaw >

MAKES 10 SERVINGS

- 1 medium head green cabbage, shredded
- 1 medium carrot, shredded
- ½ cup mayonnaise
- ½ cup milk
- ⅓ cup sugar
- 3 tablespoons lemon juice
- 1½ tablespoons white vinegar
- 1 teaspoon salt
- ⅛ teaspoon black pepper

1 Combine cabbage and carrot in large bowl; mix well.

2 Whisk mayonnaise, milk, sugar, lemon juice, vinegar, salt and pepper in medium bowl until well blended. Add to cabbage mixture; stir until blended.

Spanish Rice

MAKES 6 TO 8 SERVINGS

- 1 tablespoon olive oil
- 1 small onion, chopped
- 2 cloves garlic, minced
- 2 cups uncooked brown rice, rinsed well and drained
- 3½ cups water or chicken broth
- 1 can (about 14 ounces) diced tomatoes with green chiles
- 1½ teaspoons salt

1 Heat oil in medium saucepan over medium-high heat. Add onion and garlic; cook and stir 2 minutes. Add rice; cook and stir 2 minutes.

2 Stir in water, tomatoes and salt; bring to a boil. Reduce heat to low; cover and simmer 35 to 40 minutes or until rice is tender and water is absorbed. Fluff rice with fork.

Pineapple Upside Down Cake

MAKES 10 SERVINGS

Topping

- 1 small pineapple*
- ¼ cup (½ stick) butter
- ½ cup packed brown sugar
- Maraschino cherries

**Or substitute 7 slices of canned pineapple and proceed with step 2 after preparing pan.*

Cake

- 2 cups all-purpose flour
- 2 teaspoons baking powder
- ½ teaspoon baking soda
- ½ teaspoon salt
- ½ cup (1 stick) butter, softened
- 1 cup granulated sugar
- 1 egg
- 1 teaspoon vanilla
- 1 cup buttermilk

1. Preheat oven to 350°F. Spray 9-inch round baking pan with nonstick cooking spray. Remove top and bottom of pineapple. Cut off outside of pineapple and remove eyes. Cut pineapple crosswise into ¼-inch slices. Remove core with ½-inch cookie cutter or sharp knife.
2. For topping, cook and stir ¼ cup butter and brown sugar in medium skillet over medium heat until melted and smooth. Remove from heat. Pour into prepared pan. Arrange pineapple slices in pan, placing cherries in centers of pineapple and between slices. Reserve remaining pineapple for another use.
3. Combine flour, baking powder, baking soda and salt in medium bowl. Beat ½ cup butter and granulated sugar in large bowl with electric mixer on medium speed until well blended. Beat in egg and vanilla. Add flour mixture alternately with buttermilk, mixing on low speed just until blended after each addition. Pour batter over pineapple.
4. Bake about 1 hour or until toothpick inserted into center comes out clean. Cool in pan on wire rack 10 minutes. Run thin knife around edge of pan to loosen cake. Invert onto serving plate. Cool completely.

Note

The cake can also be baked in a 12-inch cast iron skillet. Melt the butter and brown sugar in the skillet, add the pineapple and cherries and pour the batter over the fruit. Check the cake for doneness at 40 minutes.

Peach Melba Dump Cake >

MAKES 12 TO 16 SERVINGS

- 2 cans (21 ounces each) peach pie filling
- 1 package (12 ounces) frozen raspberries, thawed and drained
- 1 package (about 15 ounces) yellow cake mix
- ½ cup (1 stick) butter, cut into thin slices
- Ice cream (optional)

1 Preheat oven to 350°F. Spray 13×9-inch baking pan with nonstick cooking spray.

2 Spread peach pie filling in prepared pan; sprinkle with raspberries. Top evenly with cake mix. Top with butter in single layer, covering cake mix as much as possible.

3 Bake 40 to 45 minutes or until toothpick inserted into center of cake comes out clean. Cool at least 15 minutes. Serve with ice cream, if desired.

Super Fudgy Brownies

MAKES 16 BROWNIES

- ½ cup all-purpose flour
- ½ cup unsweetened cocoa powder
- ½ teaspoon salt
- ½ cup (1 stick) butter
- 1 cup sugar
- 2 eggs
- 1 teaspoon vanilla
- ¾ cup semisweet or bittersweet chocolate chips

1 Preheat oven to 350°F. Line 8-inch square baking pan with parchment paper; spray with nonstick cooking spray. Sift flour, cocoa and salt into small bowl.

2 Melt butter in medium saucepan over medium heat. Remove from heat; add sugar and whisk 2 minutes. Add eggs and vanilla; whisk 1 minute or until very well blended. Add flour mixture; stir just until blended. Stir in chocolate chips. Spread batter in prepared pan; smooth top.

3 Bake 20 to 22 minutes or until edges are set and toothpick inserted into center comes out with moist crumbs. Cool completely in pan on wire rack. Remove from pan using parchment; cut into bars.

Super Simple Cheesy Bubble Loaf

MAKES 12 SERVINGS

- 2 packages (12 ounces each) refrigerated buttermilk biscuits (10 biscuits per package)
- 2 tablespoons butter, melted
- 1½ cups (6 ounces) shredded Italian cheese blend

1 Preheat oven to 350°F. Spray 9×5-inch loaf pan with nonstick cooking spray.

2 Separate biscuits; cut each biscuit into four pieces with scissors. Layer half of biscuit pieces in prepared pan. Drizzle with 1 tablespoon butter; sprinkle with 1 cup cheese. Top with remaining biscuit pieces, 1 tablespoon butter and ½ cup cheese.

3 Bake 25 minutes or until golden brown. Serve warm.

Tip

It's easy to change up the flavors in this simple bread. Try Mexican cheese blend instead of Italian, and add taco seasoning mix and/or hot pepper sauce to the melted butter before drizzling it over the dough.

Blueberry Cinnamon Dump Cake

MAKES 12 TO 16 SERVINGS

- 2 packages (12 ounces each) frozen blueberries, thawed and drained *or* 4½ cups fresh blueberries
- ⅓ cup sugar
- ¾ teaspoon ground cinnamon, divided
- 1 package (about 15 ounces) yellow cake mix
- ¾ cup (1½ sticks) butter, cut into thin slices
- Ice cream (optional)

1. Preheat oven to 350°F. Spray 13×9-inch baking pan with nonstick cooking spray.
2. Spread blueberries in prepared pan. Sprinkle with sugar and ½ teaspoon cinnamon; toss to coat. Top with cake mix, spreading evenly. Top with butter in single layer, covering cake mix as much as possible. Sprinkle with remaining ¼ teaspoon cinnamon.
3. Bake 50 to 60 minutes or until toothpick inserted into center of cake comes out clean. Cool at least 15 minutes. Serve with ice cream, if desired.

Index

Index

Index

Index

Metric Conversion Chart

VOLUME MEASUREMENTS (dry)

1/8 teaspoon = 0.5 mL
1/4 teaspoon = 1 mL
1/2 teaspoon = 2 mL
3/4 teaspoon = 4 mL
1 teaspoon = 5 mL
1 tablespoon = 15 mL
2 tablespoons = 30 mL
1/4 cup = 60 mL
1/3 cup = 75 mL
1/2 cup = 125 mL
2/3 cup = 150 mL
3/4 cup = 175 mL
1 cup = 250 mL
2 cups = 1 pint = 500 mL
3 cups = 750 mL
4 cups = 1 quart = 1 L

VOLUME MEASUREMENTS (fluid)

1 fluid ounce (2 tablespoons) = 30 mL
4 fluid ounces (1/2 cup) = 125 mL
8 fluid ounces (1 cup) = 250 mL
12 fluid ounces (1 1/2 cups) = 375 mL
16 fluid ounces (2 cups) = 500 mL

WEIGHTS (mass)

1/2 ounce = 15 g
1 ounce = 30 g
3 ounces = 90 g
4 ounces = 120 g
8 ounces = 225 g
10 ounces = 285 g
12 ounces = 360 g
16 ounces = 1 pound = 450 g

DIMENSIONS

1/16 inch = 2 mm
1/8 inch = 3 mm
1/4 inch = 6 mm
1/2 inch = 1.5 cm
3/4 inch = 2 cm
1 inch = 2.5 cm

OVEN TEMPERATURES

250°F = 120°C
275°F = 140°C
300°F = 150°C
325°F = 160°C
350°F = 180°C
375°F = 190°C
400°F = 200°C
425°F = 220°C
450°F = 230°C

BAKING PAN SIZES

Utensil	Size in Inches/Quarts	Metric Volume	Size in Centimeters
Baking or Cake Pan (square or rectangular)	8×8×2	2 L	20×20×5
	9×9×2	2.5 L	23×23×5
	12×8×2	3 L	30×20×5
	13×9×2	3.5 L	33×23×5
Loaf Pan	8×4×3	1.5 L	20×10×7
	9×5×3	2 L	23×13×7
Round Layer Cake Pan	8×1½	1.2 L	20×4
	9×1½	1.5 L	23×4
Pie Plate	8×1¼	750 mL	20×3
	9×1¼	1 L	23×3
Baking Dish or Casserole	1 quart	1 L	—
	1½ quart	1.5 L	—
	2 quart	2 L	—